# COOK IT IN A CASSEROLE

This is not a portrait of the author. She doesn't wear such a high hat when she cooks. It is Hendrik Willem Van Loon's portrait of himself, with his favorite casserole.

# COOK IT
# IN A CASSEROLE

WITH CHAFING DISH RECIPES AND MENUS

## FLORENCE BROBECK

M. BARROWS AND COMPANY, INC.

## TO THE GIFTED
HARD-WORKING IMAGINATIVE WOMEN

in the Bureau of Home Economics of the Department of Agriculture, the Extension Service workers, to the many in State Experiment Stations widely scattered throughout the country, and to those women in the great test kitchens of America's food and home appliance companies, and in the associations and publicity organizations representing such manufacturers, growers, and shippers.

The number of these nutrition-trained workers is legion. To them, American homemakers owe thanks for many thousands of recipes for good dishes using our native cheese, the citrus fruits of California and Florida, the dried fruits, avocados, nuts, and other products of the West Coast, the unsurpassed meats and meat products of the plains and the great stockyard centers, the shrimp and oysters and fish, the cereals, vegetables, dairy products, the flour, spices, bananas, pineapples, chocolate, condiments, coffee, tea, and hundreds of other supplies which are grown on this continent or have reached our kitchens from South America and the far corners of the earth.

Better ranges and refrigerators; handsome, light, airy, clean, gay, and easily-cared-for kitchens; new cookery wares; a new attitude about the one-time drudgery of homemaking—meal planning, cooking, and dishwashing every day, year after year—these are some of the results of extended laboratory and kitchen research. Radio, newspapers, big-circulation women's magazines, the decorating and fashion publications, cookery journals, many cookbooks, booklets, and free circulars have carried this new era in homemaking to American women.

The work of these scientists, nutritionists, home economists, and cooks has made a significant contribution to the evolution of America's standard of living.

# HENDRIK WILLEM VAN LOON EN CASSEROLE

*Dear Florence:*

*I am delighted about your casserole book. People sometimes ask me whether there are absolutely no mitigating circumstances for Adolf Hitler and I invariably answer, "No, not a single one!" and every day there is new proof of my contention that for absolute inhumanity, the little Corporal stands alone and is a very bad edition of the unspeakable Genghis Khan.*

*But now I am beginning to have my doubts. The Nazi leader, without in the least knowing what he was doing, is bestowing one blessing upon the people of the United States. He is forcing us to return to the oldest and the most satisfactory mode of cooking. He has brought us back to revere and respect the casserole—that earthen jar which from now on is to be the mainstay of the American family's intention to live well and feed itself in an interesting and amusing fashion until the scourge of Hitlerism shall once more have been removed from the face of a rejoicing globe. And by then, we as a nation shall have so thoroughly learned the lesson of cooking in the casserole-fashion that we shall never ask for anything else because there is not anything else that is better.*

*Therefore good luck to your little book—and I have hit upon something composed of beets, mashed potatoes, ham leftovers, celery and spices which I will let you taste the next time you visit us.*

*As ever yours,*

*Hendrik Willem van Loon.*

*Nieuw Veere*
OLD GREENWICH, CONNECTICUT

# CONTENTS

# ILLUSTRATIONS

*Photographs Courtesy Home Economics Department*
*Kraft Cheese Company and Sealtest Kitchen*

# ONE CASSEROLE—OR A DOZEN

The shopwindows in the large cities during the war years blossomed with new bouquets of cookery wares, groups of colorful casseroles of every possible shape and size to satisfy the kitchen needs of a large family or the extreme opposite of this happy household—the lone bachelor, the kitchenette household for two, and the small city apartment where a busy woman executive keeps house with one eye on her office and the other on the hospitality she feels the urge to provide for her constantly extending list of friends.

Why this sudden interest in casseroles? The obvious first answer was the shortage of the metals which formerly went into the nation's pots and pans, and during the war years was in demand elsewhere.

The second, and not so immediately obvious, reason was that America had become more nutrition-conscious during the war. Government specialists threw up their hands in horror at the large number of army draftees turned down for lack of healthy bodies—properly nourished bodies—in this the world's garden spot where anything and everything grows in wasteful abundance. Immediately the wheels in the Department of Agriculture, the Bureau of Home Economics and Nutrition, and a good many other departments were set turning. Almost overnight, housekeepers were deluged with facts about family diet, with menus which should serve as guides in feeding the family, with tables of figures, with menus and recipes for war workers and their lunch boxes and for the meals the factories offered them throughout the day in canteens and in the nurseries for workers' children.

America took another look at its gardens and its pantry shelves, its refrigerators and its milkmen's supplies. Rationing was no deterrent to the new ambition to be well fed and healthy. Instead, with the customary energy with which this country tackles any problem, American homemakers went at the family feeding problem.

Using leftovers (if any!) became essential; buying hitherto little-known cuts of meats; making whatever vegetables and fruits the grocerman had fit into menus; giving more attention to the foods which were not rationed; considering the merits of rationed canned, quick-frozen, and packaged foods more carefully than ever because points became as important as dollars—these were wartime tasks for every homemaker.

Also, labor-saving and time-saving were of primary interest to thousands of women who were giving part of each day to some war relief service or were employed, either because the men-folk were with the fighting forces and it was necessary to earn, or because, following a patriotic urge, they decided to help the labor shortage in a near-by munitions, airplane, or machine plant.

Family meals had to be served at unusual times to meet war workers' schedules; some had to be cooked quickly; some had to be prepared the night before and left ready to be popped into an oven or onto a range as soon as the cook had finished her day of making parachutes.

Schemes to combine kitchen operations became doubly important. Many casserole meals are complete: meat, fish, or chicken, with vegetables in the one dish—a salad, hot beverage, and some kind of dessert being the easily assembled additions. This saves dishwashing and table service because the casserole is brought from the oven to the table.

These same virtues have made this form of cookery welcome in the kitchenette household where there is little storage space for pots and pans, where dining, more times than not, is in the living room and the cook is maid and hostess at the same time.

A less obvious reason for the increased interest in a form of cookery very old in France and other European countries, is that many American women learned more during the war about their sisters in the occupied countries; they read more about them and their ways of living. American homemakers were both materially helpful in relief projects and loyally sympathetic in seeking out the products of those countries and using them in their own homes. Fortunately America had a good supply of French casseroles—some which probably date back many years to a time when emigrating French cooks (professional and otherwise) insisted on bringing their favorite cooking utensils with them to the new world just as all good Russians brought their samovars.

These fine old casseroles were copied by a few American firms and had a modest sale throughout the years; French firms in America specialized in their native kitchen equipment to supply Parisian and Alsatian chefs in hotels and restaurants, and some of these restaurant supplies found their way into family homes.

After the repeal of the prohibition amendment, when there was a concerted drive in this country to interest women as well as men in wines both domestic and imported, all phases of gourmet cookery were publicized through the superbly edited home decorating and gardening magazines and the smart fashion journals. It was suddenly chic to know how to cook. Socially prominent names headed the culinary and restaurant-reporting columns of these magazines as well as of other publications.

All of this aided in creating a demand for casseroles, for many of the gourmet dishes described by such writers called for casserole cookery. When imports ended with the beginning of war, the American manufacturers promptly stepped forward with excellent copies of French earthenware baking dishes and with some new designs of their own.

The result is that today there is an almost overwhelming supply of handsome oven cookery ware in excellent American-made glass, of course, which has been with us many years now, and in glazed earthen baking dishes, round, oblong, deep, shallow, for top-of-the-stove cooking as well as snug in a friendly oven. In addition to the baked-earth brown color familiar in all European casseroles, the models we use today, besides glass, are blackish brown and highly glazed, or they are green or white or almost any color to match kitchen schemes and tableware. Gifted designers have created beautiful color combinations in some of this ovenware, so handsome that it is sold alongside rare silver in the country's best shops.

From five-and-ten baking dishes (made by nationally known companies in spite of its low prices) and the twenty-five-cent and chain-department store supplies to the superbly beautiful pieces sold in fine shops, and the astounding array available in the big housewares stores and in most department stores, there are casseroles for every kind of kitchen.

The old hands at this cookery issue one important warning: Read the directions that come with the new dish as to its care and use.

Culled from the labels of most of the wares on the sales counters these days are these reminders:

Do not place a cold casserole or a casserole of cold food in a hot oven. Extreme changes of temperature should be avoided.

Do not put cold food (such as butter or milk) from the refrigerator into a hot casserole.

Do not handle a hot casserole with a wet cloth or place the hot baking dish on a cold or wet surface, such as a sink top.

Much of the "flame" ware made of earthenware and pottery should be used with an asbestos mat beneath the dish. For this top-of-the-stove cooking the dish should be heated gradually and never used with extremely high heat. When the food in it has begun to cook, reduce the heat for best results in flavor and for economy of fuel.

Do not place the utensil on the heat without food in it.

Shop for casseroles on the ensemble plan. Most of them are made in sets of several sizes in varied and useful shapes. If you are serving a casserole meal (it is usually easy to cook two or three things at once in the oven), it is a nice touch in table color scheming to have all the casseroles of the same finish and color. The very large, deep soup casseroles are awkward on the table but a joy on a serving table or wheeled wagon rolled from the range to a place within reach of your chair. The soup stays hot throughout the meal, and when the whole lunch or supper is made on this dish (with salad, coffee, and a sweet) having the casserole of hot soup at hand makes it easy to refill the dishes of the hungry guests.

Once having acquired a casserole, you will quickly see the need of another one. With two or more in your kitchen, meal planning takes a turn for the better. Almost any leftover, popped into a casserole, topped with a sauce and crumbs, becomes with the blessing of the oven heat a gourmet concoction.

## MENUS

The menus which follow show only a few of the possible uses of the recipes given in this book, and they are intended only as suggestions—general guides for anyone using the book. What you can find at the market and the grocery store or in the garden, what is on your supply shelves and in the refrigerator, what your local bakeshops offer in bread and rolls, the personal preferences of members of the household or of invited guests will dictate changes, variations, and improvements on these menus to suit your needs.

The menus which seem too elaborate need only to have one or two courses eliminated or some more simple dish substituted. Those which seem slim call for the addition of, perhaps, another vegetable or an appetizer or soup before the meal, or a more elaborate dessert served at the end.

With most of these luncheons and suppers or dinners a hot beverage is indicated, coffee (decaffeinated coffee is popular for late suppers with an increasing number of people) or tea. In hot weather, a tall glass of iced coffee, tea, ginger ale, fruit juices, coffee and chocolate mixed, or any other preferred beverage is in order.

Dessert has been omitted from a few menus. When this is the case, either have a few unusual candies on the coffee tray or serve a sweet cordial at that time.

Most of the menus are interchangeable for luncheon, dinner, supper on Sunday night, or some other occasion when informal dining is in order. Many of them are just right for Sunday or holiday brunch when the idea is to get away from the conventional pattern of either breakfast or luncheon and to eat what you like, lingering over the coffee long afterwards.

In all menus the recipes for the main dish, salad, and dessert are given in the pages which follow. Other dishes, obvious and widely known, are mentioned in a few menus, but recipes for these are not included in this small and specialized book. They and many others which you must know for day-after-day cooking and entertaining are in the three or four general cookbooks you probably own. Read and study such books, read the authors' introductions and profit by the experience of the gifted and capable women who have put them together.

Cooking is an art and a pleasure, but it is a science as well. It is worth while to give it serious study so that ease in meal planning and cooking and in being a generous and comfortable hostess may become second nature for you. If in addition you "have a flair for food," you then are justified in spending the family money on the glorious products of the great fields and truck gardens, the poultry farms, the fisheries and meat shops, the dairies and orchards, which have helped give America its name—The Land of Plenty.

# CASSEROLE SOUP SUPPERS

Black Bean Soup
French Bread and Butter with Apricot Jam
Spring Salad Platter
Caramel Bread Pudding
Coffee

❖

Lentil Soup
Pumpernickel and Butter
Tossed Green Salad with Cheese
Lemon Crumb Pudding with Top Milk or Cream
Coffee

❖

Relish Dish of Carrot Straws, Ripe Olives, Radishes
Minestrone with Cheese
Italian Sweet Rye Bread or Bread Sticks and Butter
Spiced Pear Jam
Orange Soufflé with Custard
Coffee

❖

Mulligatawny Soup
Whole Wheat Rolls and Butter with Apple Butter
Romaine and Grapefruit Salad
Low-Sugar Chocolate Cake
Coffee

Onion Soup au Gratin
Toasted Rolls and Butter
Potato Salad and Cold Cuts
Ohio Apple Pudding with Cream or Sour Cream
Coffee

*

Pepperpot
Hot Biscuits and Butter
Endive or Romaine Salad and Cheese Tray
Baked Pears
Coffee

*

Pot-au-Feu
French Bread and Butter
Crêpes Suzette
Coffee

*

Clam Chowder with Chowder Crackers
Chicken Salad
Buttered Rolls
Hickory Nut Cake
Coffee

## BLACK BEAN SOUP

1 pint black beans
2 quarts water
1 ham bone
2 stalks celery, chopped fine
2 tablespoons flour
2 tablespoons butter
1-inch cube salt pork

½ teaspoon salt
¼ teaspoon pepper
½ teaspoon mustard
¼ teaspoon paprika
1 clove garlic
3 lemons (2 squeezed, 1 sliced)
3 hard-cooked eggs

Soak beans twelve hours overnight. Put them in fresh water, add ham bone, celery, and half the butter. Simmer three hours, adding more water as it diminishes with boiling. Rub through a sieve, reheat, and add salt, pepper, mustard, and paprika. At end, add butter and flour cooked together. Stir well. Cut eggs and lemon in thin slices. Add to the soup just before serving. Serves six.

## MULLIGATAWNY SOUP

3 quarts white stock (or use
    bouillon cubes)
3 cups boiled rice
1 cup diced uncooked chicken
1 small can tomatoes, or 1 cup
    cooked tomatoes
1 sliced onion

1 sliced carrot
1 sliced heart of celery
1 chopped green pepper
½ cup butter
½ cup flour
1 teaspoon curry powder
¼ teaspoon cloves

¼ clove garlic

Heat the stock in a deep casserole. Brown onion, celery, carrot, pepper, and chicken in butter. Add flour, curry, cloves, garlic, and tomatoes, and simmer for one hour. Remove the chicken, and rub the vegetables through a sieve. Add the chicken and strained vegetables to the hot stock, season with salt and pepper, add hot rice, and serve. Serves eight to ten.

## CLAM CHOWDER

1 quart clams
2 sliced onions
6 cubed potatoes

3 slices salt pork
1 quart whole milk
2 tablespoons butter

Salt and pepper

Shuck clams, rinse in clam liquor, and remove black portions. Chop fine in a wooden mixing bowl. Cook onions and potatoes in just enough water to cover, for fifteen minutes. Then add the clams and cook another fifteen minutes. Cut salt pork in three-eighths-inch cubes, fry till brown, and drain on thick paper toweling. Add pork scraps and fat to clams and vegetables, and turn them into a casserole. Heat the milk and add it to the chowder. Add butter, and season to taste. Serves six.

## LEEK AND POTATO SOUP

1 bunch leeks
1 cup celery
3 cups potatoes, diced
Cayenne

1 quart consommé (or use
    bouillon cubes)
5 tablespoons butter
Salt and pepper

Cut leeks and celery in thin slices, and cook in butter in a casserole until soft. Add consommé, and cook forty minutes. Meanwhile, cook the potatoes for ten minutes in boiling salted water. Then drain and add to the consommé and continue cooking. Season with salt, pepper, and cayenne. Serve from the casserole. Serves four.

## LENTIL SOUP

2 cups lentils
1½ quarts water
⅔ cup rice

½ cup olive oil
2 onions
Salt and pepper

Pick over lentils, and boil three hours. Add uncooked rice, and cook till rice is done, stirring often. Turn into a casserole, add the onions chopped fine and browned in oil. Boil five minutes. Season with salt and pepper. Serves four to six.

## MINESTRONE

½ cup peas  
4 carrots  
2 potatoes  
4 stalks celery with leaves  
¼ head white cabbage  
1 onion  

1 clove garlic  
1 small bunch parsley  
2 quarts water  
1 tablespoon salt  
1 tablespoon olive oil  
Grated Parmesan cheese  

Wash and cut up vegetables. Add minced garlic and parsley. Put all in deep casserole with water and salt, and boil for two hours. Add olive oil, stir well. Sprinkle each serving generously with grated cheese. Serves six.

## ONION SOUP AU GRATIN

*Make a stock from:*  
4 pounds of beef (shin)  
1 knuckle veal  
2 onions  
1 carrot, minced  
1 stalk celery, minced  

Parsley, few leaves and stems, minced  
*Add (tied in cheesecloth):*  
6 cloves  
1 bay leaf  
6 coriander seeds (crushed)  
12 peppercorns

Allow a quart of cold water to every pound of meat; set on the back of the range (or any low-heat spot) in covered kettle, heat slowly to boiling, then increase the heat but keep the contents just at the boiling point—not boiling rapidly—until the juices have been drawn out of the meat. This will take from two to three hours. If more water is needed while simmering, use boiling water. Prepare the day before it is to be used, remove fat from the kettle; strain stock. Have ready:

12 onions, medium-sized,    French bread
   peeled               Parmesan cheese, grated
                  Butter

Peel onions, fry in butter till tender and brown. Place in the bottom of a deep casserole and cover with thin slices of toasted French bread. Cover these with grated cheese. Fill casserole with the prepared stock and cook in the oven for one hour (moderate 375 degrees F.). Serve with a piece of the toast in each dish and more cheese on each bowlful. Serves six to eight.

## PEPPERPOT

¼ cup chopped celery      ½ pound honey comb tripe, cut
½ cup chopped green peppers    fine
¼ cup chopped onion       1½ cups potatoes, diced
4 tablespoons butter       ½ teaspoon pepper
3 tablespoons flour        1 tablespoon salt
5 cups chicken stock       ½ cup cream

Cook vegetables in half the butter fifteen minutes; then add flour and stir till well mixed. Add remaining ingredients except cream. Cover and cook one-half hour. Before serving, add cream and remaining butter. Serves four.

## POT-AU-FEU

4 pounds lean beef       1 bay leaf
6 quarts cold water      5 allspice
2 cups diced turnips     2 cups diced potatoes
2 onions, sliced         Small piece lemon peel
2 cups diced carrots     4 stalks celery, chopped
1 cup diced parsnips     3 tablespoons chopped parsley
2 cloves               2 teaspoons salt
          ¼ teaspoon black pepper

Put the meat in a deep casserole (one especially for pot-au-feu) with the water around it, and heat slowly. As the scum becomes thick, remove it. After skimming well, add vegetables and seasonings, and let the pot cook slowly for five hours. Serve in the deep casserole at the table. Serves eight to ten.

## FISH DINNERS EN CASSEROLE

Tomato and Carrot Juice Cocktail
Codfish Pie
Corn Muffins and Butter with Plum Jam
Berry Loaf and Cream
Coffee

❀

Celery Hearts, Carrot Straws, Radishes
Crab Meat Casserole      Baked Potatoes
Whole Wheat Rolls and Butter
Grapefruit Apple Crisp
Coffee

❀

Halibut with Tomato Sauce
Buttered String Beans
Boston Brown Bread and Butter
Chocolate Velvet Cream
Coffee

❀

Fresh Fruit Cup
Baked Salmon and Noodles
Pumpernickel and Butter with Currant Jelly
Coconut Bread Pudding
Coffee

*Italian Fillet of Sole*
*Potatoes boiled in Jackets*
*Whole Wheat Bread and Butter*
*Coleslaw*
*Melon filled with Fruit*
*Coffee or Tea*

❋

*Swedish Fish Soufflé*
*Green Beans and Rice au Gratin*
*Swedish Crisp Bread and Butter*
*Garden Salad*
*Marvel Chocolate Pie*
*Coffee or Tea*

❋

*Country Scalloped Oysters*
*Spoon Bread and Butter*
*Artichoke Hearts and Tomato Salad*
*Cooked Mixed Fruits and Brownies*
*Coffee or Tea*

❋

*Cranberry and Orange Juice Cocktail*
*Deviled Shrimp Pie*
*Rolls and Butter*
*Tossed Green Salad*
*Butterscotch Bread Pudding*
*Coffee or Tea*

*Relish Tray of Seasoned Cottage Cheese, Carrot Straws,*
*Radishes, Green Onions, Olives*
*Shrimp Bake*
*Hot Popovers and Butter*
*Raspberry Slump*
*Coffee or Tea*

❋

*Oysters and Rice*
*Oatmeal Bread and Butter*
*Corn Pudding*
*Coleslaw garnished with Carrot Straws*
*Baked Apples*
*Coffee or Tea*

## CODFISH NEAPOLITAN

3 cups cooked spaghetti     1½ cups seasoned White Sauce
1½ cups cooked cod           Bread crumbs
Butter                       Grated cheese

In a buttered casserole, arrange a layer of the cooked spaghetti, and cover with a little of the White Sauce; then a layer of codfish, with sauce on that. Top with another layer of spaghetti and pour White Sauce over it. Sprinkle liberally with buttered crumbs and grated cheese. A few dabs of butter add to the flavor. Set in a moderate oven (375 degrees F.), and brown fifteen to twenty minutes. Serves six.

## BAKED SALMON AND NOODLES

3 cups cooked noodles     1½ cups milk
2 cups salmon             1 egg
            Buttered bread crumbs

Put one-third of the noodles seasoned with salt and pepper in a buttered baking dish. Cover with half the salmon, dot with butter. Repeat with noodles, salmon, butter, and noodles. Top with butttered crumbs and bake until browned. Serves six.

## CODFISH PIE

1 package quick-frozen fillets of cod, or 1½ cups cooked cod
2 tablespoons chopped onion
1 cup diced celery
3 tablespoons butter
¾ teaspoon salt
Dash of pepper
⅓ cup water
1¾ cups fish liquor and milk
3 tablespoons flour
½ box (1 cup) quick-frozen green peas, cooked
Pastry

Cut fish (frozen or thawed) in one-inch cubes. Cook onion and celery in one tablespoon butter, covered, five minutes. Add fish, salt, pepper, and water. Cover, and cook gently four to twelve minutes, or until done, stirring occasionally with fork. Drain, reserving liquor; add milk to make one and three-fourths cups.

Melt remaining butter in saucepan, add flour, and blend. Add liquid gradually, stirring constantly; cook and stir until thickened. Add fish mixture and peas. Turn into greased one-quart casserole. Roll pastry one-eighth-inch thick. Fit over top of casserole, making several slits to permit escape of steam. Place in a pan of hot water and bake in a hot oven (475 degrees F.) thirty minutes, or until crust is done. Serves four.

To make pastry, measure three-fourths cup sifted flour, add one-fourth teaspoon salt, and sift again. Cut in three tablespoons cold shortening until pieces are about the size of small peas. Add about four teaspoons cold water, a small amount at a time, mixing lightly with fork. Handle as little as possible. Wrap in waxed paper and chill thoroughly before using.

For cheese crust, mix one-third cup grated American cheese with flour-fat mixture.

## CRAB MEAT CASSEROLE

2 cups crab meat lumps
3 eggs, yolks and whites beaten
   separately
2 cups thick Cream Sauce, well
   seasoned

½ cup grated Swiss cheese
Salt and pepper
Cayenne

Add the cayenne, beaten egg yolks, and the grated cheese to the Cream Sauce. Beat well together. Heat the crab lumps in the upper part of a double boiler, over boiling water and, when warm, season with salt and pepper. Mix carefully with the sauce so as not to break the lumps apart too much. Fold in the egg whites beaten stiff, and pour into a buttered casserole. Set in a pan of hot water in a hot oven (400 degrees F.) for twenty minutes. Serve at once. Serves six.

## HALIBUT WITH TOMATO SAUCE

4 slices halibut, 1 inch thick
1 small can tomatoes
¼ cup chopped parsley
1 green pepper, chopped fine
1 clove garlic, chopped fine

½ pound American cheese,
   grated
1 tablespoon butter
1 teaspoon salt
½ teaspoon pepper

Heat frying pan, and fry fish lightly in the butter. Transfer to a baking dish. In a saucepan boil tomatoes, parsley, celery, pepper, and garlic together until soft. Cover the halibut with most of the grated cheese, reserving about one-fourth of the cheese. Dot the halibut with butter, add seasonings, and pour the tomato mixture over it. Bake fifteen minutes in a moderate oven (375 degrees F.), then cover the top with the remaining cheese, and leave uncovered in the oven two or three minutes longer till the cheese melts. Serve in the baking dish. Serves four.

## CRAB MEAT CASSEROLE

2 pounds flaked crab meat
2 cups milk
¼ cup butter
2 tablespoons flour
1 teaspoon salt

⅛ teaspoon pepper
1 well-beaten egg
2 hard-boiled eggs
3 tablespoons sherry
Buttered bread crumbs

Bring milk to boiling in a double boiler. Melt butter and add flour and seasonings to it; then add this to milk just before it boils. Stir, let it thicken, and then let it cool. Add beaten egg and hard-boiled eggs mashed with the sherry. Mix with the crab meat. Pour mixture into a casserole, top with crumbs, and bake twenty minutes in a hot (400 degrees F.) oven. Serves six.

## SCALLOPED FISH

1 pound fish
Bread crumbs
1½ cups White Sauce, seasoned
    with

¼ teaspoon mace and
½ teaspoon paprika

Boil the fish, let cool in the same water. When cold, take out all bones and break up the fish in small pieces, but do not mince it.

Put alternate layers of fish and seasoned White Sauce in a well-buttered casserole. Cover top with crumbs. Set in a hot oven (400 degrees F.) till browned and bubbly. Serves four to five.

## FISH SCALLOP

½ pound cooked haddock
    (or other fish)
1 tablespoon flour
1 tablespoon butter

2 eggs, hard cooked, yolks only
½ teaspoon salt
⅔ cup milk
1 teaspoon lemon juice

1 tablespoon chopped parsley

Mince fish coarsely. Make a thick sauce by melting the butter and stirring the flour into it smoothly, gradually adding the milk; stir while it thickens; then add fish and yolks of eggs mashed fine, parsley, a little salt and pepper, and the lemon juice. Put in small casserole or baking dish, sprinkle with crumbs, and bake in a hot oven (400 degrees F.) till browned. Serves four.

## CREAMED BAKED LOBSTER

1 cup butter  
1 cup flour  
1 quart rich milk  
Salt and pepper

1 lemon  
2 pounds flaked lobster  
2 eggs, slightly beaten  
Bread crumbs

Make a white sauce by melting the butter, stirring the flour into it smoothly, and adding the milk gradually, stirring all the while till medium thick. Squeeze the juice of the lemon over the lobster meat. Add the beaten eggs and salt and pepper to the white sauce, and pour at once over the lobster. Turn into a baking dish and top with bread crumbs which have been dipped in melted butter. Set in moderate oven (375 degrees F.) till browned. Serves eight.

## ALSATIAN SOLE

1 pound fillets of sole  
2½ cups sauerkraut

1 cup Mornay Sauce  
Grated cheese  
¾ cup white wine

Poach the sole in the wine in a glass or enameled saucepan till tender and done. Braise the sauerkraut in a saucepan, and arrange a layer of the kraut in the bottom of a baking dish. Arrange the cooked sole on this, cover with the Mornay Sauce, sprinkle with grated cheese, and brown quickly in a hot oven (450 degrees F.). Serves four.

## SOLE WITH HERBS

1 pound fillets of sole  
1 cup vegetable-marrow, chopped  
Parsley, few leaves and stems  
Rosemary and basil, a crumble of each  
Bread crumbs  
Butter  
Lemon juice

Cook the minced vegetable-marrows and roughly chopped parsley in butter, adding a very small amount of chopped rosemary and basil. Lay the fillets of sole in a buttered shallow baking dish, cover with the cooked mixture, sprinkle with buttered bread crumbs, and pour on a few tablespoons of melted butter. Cook in a moderate oven (375 degrees F.) till the fish is tender and done. On serving, add a little lemon juice and chopped parsley. Serves four.

## TUNA CASSEROLE

4 cold boiled potatoes, cubed  
¼ cup melted butter  
1½ cups cooked peas  
2 small cans tuna fish  
2 tablespoons butter  
2 tablespoons flour  
1¾ cups milk  
1 pound mild cheese, grated  
Salt and pepper

Before using canned tuna fish, place the fish in a colander and pour boiling water over it to remove the oil. Put potatoes, peas, melted butter, and fish in a buttered baking dish. Make a cheese sauce by melting two tablespoons butter and stirring the two tablespoons of flour smoothly into it, adding milk gradually; let thicken a little, add seasonings and cheese. Stir smoothly. Pour over the mixture in the casserole and top with buttered bread crumbs. Bake forty-five minutes in a moderate oven (375 degrees F.). Serves six.

## ITALIAN FILLET OF SOLE

| | |
|---|---|
| 1 pound fillets of sole | Salt and pepper |
| 1 slice onion | Boiled spinach (about 2 cups) |
| Parsley | Cayenne |
| 1 cup white wine, or white grape juice with squeeze of lemon | 4 tablespoons cheese, grated |
| | 1 cup White Sauce |

Remove the skin from the fillets and boil gently for ten minutes with the wine and seasonings. Cover well. When tender, remove and place in a baking dish on a layer of cooked spinach which has been minced and tossed in butter with one tablespoon grated onion.

To the White Sauce add one-half cup of the broth from the fish kettle, a dash of cayenne, and one tablespoon of grated cheese. Pour this over the fish, sprinkle lightly with grated cheese and brown in a moderate oven (375 degrees F.). Serves four to five.

## SWEDISH FISH SOUFFLÉ

| | |
|---|---|
| ⅓ cup butter | ½ tablespoon butter (extra) |
| ½ cup flour | 4 eggs |
| 2 cups milk | Salt |
| 2 cups cooked fish | White pepper |
| 2 tablespoons bread crumbs | ½ teaspoon vinegar |

Make a white sauce of the butter, flour, and milk; cook for five minutes, then let it cool. Add to it the cooked, finely chopped fish and the beaten egg yolks. Season. Have the egg whites stiffly beaten and fold into the fish mixture. Pour into a buttered and bread-crumbed casserole. Set in a pan of hot water and bake in a moderate oven (385 degrees F.) for thirty minutes. Serve with melted butter. Serves eight.

## BAKED OYSTERS AND MACARONI

1 pint oysters  
1½ cups boiled macaroni  
Salt and pepper

½ cup buttered bread crumbs  
½ cup grated cheese  
¼ cup butter

Put a layer of macaroni in the bottom of a buttered casserole, cover with the oysters, sprinkle with salt and pepper and some of the grated cheese, and dot with butter. Repeat, and cover the top with buttered crumbs. Set in a hot oven (425 degrees F.) for twenty minutes. Serves six.

## COUNTRY SCALLOPED OYSTERS

36 oysters  
1 cup oyster liquor  
1 cup cream

¼ cup butter  
Salt and pepper  
Bread crumbs

Put a layer of oysters in a buttered baking dish and cover with a half-inch layer of dry bread crumbs. Sprinkle with salt and pepper, then add a second layer of oysters. Repeat, covering with a thin layer of crumbs, dots of butter, and seasoning. Repeat until the dish is filled. The top layers of oysters should be well covered with crumbs and butter. Pour the oyster liquor and cream over all. Bake in a hot oven (400 degrees F.) for twenty minutes or until browned. Serves six.

## OYSTERS AND RICE

1 green pepper  
1 onion, peeled  
⅓ cup butter  
¾ cup rice

2½ cups bouillon or water  
4 tomatoes, peeled and seeded  
1 teaspoon salt  
1 pint to 1 quart oysters

3 slices bacon

Parboil the pepper, remove seeds and membranes, and chop. Add to chopped onion and cook in butter until yellowed. Blanch the rice, put in a casserole with the onion, pepper, bouillon, tomatoes, and salt, and stir until the rice is nearly tender and the liquid cooked down. Set it in a low oven for this (300 degrees F.). Meanwhile pick over and wash the oysters. Stir into the cooked rice and continue cooking fifteen minutes or until the oysters are plump and edges curled. Top the casserole for the last fifteen minutes with chopped bacon which has been browned. Serves six to eight.

## OYSTER CHOWDER

2 slices diced fat bacon
2 chopped onions
2 stalks minced celery
6 potatoes, sliced
1 teaspoon salt

¼ teaspoon pepper
1 pint milk
1 pint cream
2 tablespoons butter
1 tablespoon flour

1 pint oysters

Fry out bacon, remove from the pan, and add onions, celery, potatoes, and seasonings. Cover with boiling water and cook until the potatoes are almost tender. Turn into a casserole, add milk and cream; heat to boiling, then thicken with blended flour and butter. Stir smoothly. Add oysters and cook until the edges curl or the oysters are puffed up fat. Serves four to six.

## OYSTER STEW

2 to 2½ dozen small oysters
Milk

4 tablespoons butter
Salt and pepper

Oyster crackers

Drain the oysters and pick them over for bits of shell. Strain the liquid and measure it. Cook oysters in liquid until the edges begin to curl. Measure enough milk to make a total of six cups of liquid in all. Scald milk, add oysters, oyster liquid, and butter, and season with salt and pepper. Reheat in the casserole and serve at once with oyster crackers. Six servings.

## SCALLOPED OYSTERS AND SCALLOPS

1 quart oysters
1 pint scallops
¾ cup cream
¼ cup oyster liquor

2 cups bread crumbs
½ cup butter, melted
1 teaspoon salt
⅛ teaspoon pepper

Mix melted butter and bread crumbs together, and put a thin layer in the bottom of a large greased casserole. Cover with oysters and seasonings; add some cream and oyster liquor. Add a layer of scallops, seasonings, and crumbs; then a layer of oysters and liquids. Top with scallops and bread crumbs, and bake in a hot oven (425 degrees F.) thirty minutes. Serves eight to ten.

## DEVILED SHRIMP PIE

3 tablespoons butter
2 tablespoons flour
1 cup milk
½ teaspoon dry mustard
¼ teaspoon salt

¼ teaspoon paprika
Dash of cayenne
2 tablespoons chopped parsley
1 tablespoon lemon juice
2 No. 1 cans shrimp

2 cups fluffy mashed potatoes

Make a white sauce of the butter, flour, and milk, stirring constantly. Cook until thickened. Add mustard, salt, paprika, cayenne, chopped parsley, lemon juice, and cleaned shrimp. Fill a nine-inch glass pie pan. Make a border around the edge of the pan with the potatoes (use pastry tube or spoon). Bake in a moderate oven (375 degrees F.) twenty minutes, until potatoes are lightly browned. Makes eight servings.

## SCALLOPED EGGS AND SHRIMP

4 tablespoons butter
4 tablespoons flour
2 cups milk
½ teaspoon salt
Dash of cayenne

2 tablespoons chopped
pimiento
1 tablespoon chopped parsley
4 hard-cooked eggs
2 No. 1 cans shrimp

1 cup buttered soft bread crumbs

Make a white sauce of the butter, flour, and milk, stirring constantly. Cook until thickened. Add salt, cayenne, chopped pimiento, and parsley. Slice eggs. Arrange alternate layers of sliced eggs and cleaned shrimp in buttered casserole. Add sauce. Top with buttered bread crumbs. Bake in moderate oven (375 degrees F.) twenty minutes, until crumbs are browned. Makes eight servings.

## SHRIMP PIE

1½ pounds fresh shrimp
1 pint stewed tomatoes
3 onions, chopped
2 tablespoons butter

2 tablespoons flour
2 hard-boiled eggs
½ cup stuffed olives
6 boiled onions

Boil fresh shrimp twenty minutes in salted water. Let cool in the same water, then remove the shells and the dark vein from each. Rinse in clear water. (Canned shrimp may be used; remove the dark vein, and rinse.)

Fry chopped onions in butter until brown; then stir in tomatoes, flour, and shrimp, and cook together for three minutes. Line a deep pie dish with rich pastry, put boiled onions around the sides. Pour in the shrimp mixture, and slice eggs and olives over the top. Cover with pie crust and bake forty-five minutes in a moderate oven (375 degrees F.). Serves six.

## MISSISSIPPI SHRIMP PIE

5 tablespoons butter
5 tablespoons flour
3¾ cups milk
2 No. 1 cans shrimp
1¼ cups cooked peas

1 teaspoon salt
⅛ teaspoon pepper
3 tablespoons chopped green
    pepper
2 hard-cooked eggs, diced

Baking powder biscuit dough

Make a white sauce of the butter, flour, and milk, stirring con-stantly, and cook until thickened. Add cleaned shrimp, peas, salt, pepper, green pepper, and diced eggs. Pour into casserole. Top with baking powder biscuits. Bake in hot oven (425 degrees F.) thirty minutes. Makes eight to ten servings.

## SHRIMP AND RICE CASSEROLE

3 tablespoons butter
4 tablespoons flour
2½ cups tomato juice
1 teaspoon salt

Dash of cayenne
2 No. 1 cans shrimp
1¼ cups cooked peas
1½ cups cooked rice

1 cup buttered bread crumbs

Melt butter, blend in flour, add tomato juice, stirring con-stantly, and cook until thickened. Add salt and cayenne. Add cleaned shrimp, peas, and rice. Place in buttered casserole and top with buttered bread crumbs. Bake in moderate oven (375 degrees F.) twenty-five minutes. Makes eight servings.

## SHRIMP SOUFFLÉ

3 tablespoons butter
4 tablespoons flour
½ teaspoon salt

1 cup milk
1 No. 1 can shrimp
3 egg yolks

3 egg whites

Make a white sauce of the butter, flour, salt, and milk, stirring constantly. Cook until thickened. Shred the cleaned shrimp and add to the sauce. Cool. Beat egg yolks; add. Beat egg whites stiff and fold into the shrimp mixture. Pour into the baking dish, set in a pan of hot water, and bake in a moderate oven (350 degrees F.) fifty minutes. Serve immediately. Makes six servings.

## SHRIMP AND MACARONI

1 eight-ounce package maca-
    roni
5 tablespoons butter
5 tablespoons chopped green
    pepper
1 cup grated American cheese

4 tablespoons flour
2⅔ cups milk
½ teaspoon salt
Dash of cayenne
1 No. 1 can shrimp

Cook macaroni in boiling salted water until tender; drain. Melt butter in saucepan, add green pepper, and cook ten minutes. Push pepper to one side of saucepan; blend in flour. Add milk, stirring constantly, and cook until thickened; add remaining ingredients and drained macaroni. Turn into buttered casserole. Bake in moderate oven (375 degrees F.) thirty minutes. Makes eight servings.

## SHRIMP AND RICE AU GRATIN

2 tablespoons butter
3 tablespoons flour
1⅔ cups tomato juice
½ teaspoon salt
Dash of cayenne

1 cup grated American cheese
1 No. 1 can shrimp
1¼ cups cooked rice
1 cup soft bread crumbs
2 tablespoons melted butter

Melt butter, blend in flour. Add tomato juice, stirring constantly, and cook until thickened. Add salt, cayenne, and grated American cheese; stir until cheese is melted. Add cleaned shrimp and rice. Place in casserole and cover with crumbs which have been mixed with the melted butter. Bake in a moderate oven (375 degrees F.) fifteen minutes, until crumbs are brown. Makes eight servings.

## SHRIMP BAKE

2 No. 1 cans shrimp
3 medium onions, sliced
2 green peppers, cut in rings
1½ cups cooked peas
¼ teaspoon salt

1⅓ cups coarsely broken wide noodles, uncooked
3½ cups cooked tomatoes with juice
4 tablespoons butter
½ teaspoon pepper

Place alternate layers of shrimp, noodles, and mixed vegetables in a casserole. Dot with butter, and season with salt and pepper. Cover and bake in moderate oven (350 degrees F.) one hour. Makes eight servings.

## SHRIMP TOMATO CASSEROLE

1 No. 1 can shrimp
3½ cups half-inch bread cubes (about 6 slices)
3 eggs, slightly beaten

1 teaspoon salt
⅛ teaspoon pepper
2½ cups tomatoes
⅔ cup grated cheese

Combine shrimp and cubed bread. Put in a buttered one-and-one-half-quart casserole. Beat eggs slightly, add salt, pepper, and tomatoes. Pour over shrimp and bread. Sprinkle top with grated cheese. Bake in a moderate oven (350 degrees F.) forty-five minutes. Makes eight servings.

# EGGS IN CASSEROLE MENUS

Small Casserole Baked Onion Soup
Shirred Eggs in Macaroni
Buttered String Beans
Toasted French Bread and Butter
Fresh Berries and Cream
Coffee or Tea

❀

Chilled Pineapple Juice
Egg Casserole    Baked Lima Beans
Buttered Toast
Tossed Green Salad
Orange Refrigerator Cake
Coffee or Tea

❀

Tomato Bouillon
Eggs Marguerite
Buttered Asparagus
Toasted Rolls and Butter with Blackberry Jam
Orange Soufflé
Coffee or Tea

❀

Baked Eggs Mornay
Crisp Bacon    Toasted Rolls
Cranberry Relish and Endive Salad
Stewed Fruits
Coffee

*Creole Baked Eggs*
*Peas Breton*
*Popovers and Butter*
*Fresh Pineapple Slices*
*Coffee or Tea*

\*

*Eggs and Potatoes*
*Scalloped Tomatoes*
*Whole Wheat Rolls and Butter*
*Avocado Pear with Special Dressing*
*Orange Sherbet and Cookies*
*Coffee*

## BAKED EGGS MORNAY

6 eggs
1½ cups Mornay Sauce

1 cup soft bread crumbs
1 tablespoon melted butter

Rub a shallow casserole with butter. Break the eggs and slip them carefully into the dish. Cover with the sauce and then sprinkle with crumbs mixed with the butter. Bake in a moderate oven (375 degrees F.) about fifteen minutes, till the eggs are firm. Serves six.

## EGGS AND POTATOES

3 cups hot mashed potatoes
2 tablespoons chopped chives

6 eggs
1 tablespoon butter

Paprika, salt, and pepper

Add chives to potatoes and beat well. Spread in a buttered shallow baking dish, and make six hollows in the potatoes. Into each, drop an egg. Dot with butter, season with a little salt and pepper. Set in a moderate oven (375 degrees F.) about fifteen minutes, till the eggs are firm. Serves six.

## CREOLE BAKED EGGS

6 eggs
½ cup bread crumbs
½ cup grated cheese
¼ teaspoon salt

4 tablespoons butter
3 tablespoons chopped green pepper
3 tablespoons chopped onion

1 cup strained, mashed canned or cooked tomatoes

Melt butter in a frying pan, add pepper, onion, and tomatoes, and cook until slightly browned. Pour into a shallow baking dish. Break the eggs onto this mixture. Season the eggs. Mix cheese, crumbs, and salt, and sprinkle thickly over the eggs. Bake in a moderate oven (375 degrees F.) for fifteen minutes, until the eggs are firm. Serves six.

## EGG CASSEROLE

6 hard-cooked eggs
2 small onions, chopped fine
1 cup ham, chopped fine
6 medium-sized mushrooms, chopped fine

2 tablespoons Cream Sauce
2 cups Cheese Sauce
Salt and pepper
Grated cheese

Cut the hard-cooked eggs in half lengthwise and remove the yolks. Pan-fry the onions, ham, and mushrooms in butter. Crush the egg yolks with a fork, and add them with the Cream Sauce to the onion, ham, and mushroom mixture. Fill the egg whites with the cooked mixture and cover with Cheese Sauce in a casserole. Sprinkle with a few spoonfuls of grated cheese, and bake in a hot oven (400 degrees F.) ten to fifteen minutes, until thoroughly heated. Serves six.

## EGGS MARGUERITE

| | |
|---|---|
| 1 cup cream | Cheese, thinly sliced |
| 6 eggs | Salt and pepper |
| 1 tablespoon butter | Cayenne |

Put the butter in a glass or earthenware shirred-egg dish or any shallow casserole. When melted enough to cover the bottom of the dish, add one-half cup of cream seasoned with salt and pepper; then add a thin layer of cheese. Break eggs carefully into the dish, pour the rest of the cream over them; add seasonings and another thin layer of cheese; bake for twenty minutes in a slow oven (250 degrees F.). Serves six.

## SHIRRED EGGS IN MACARONI

| | |
|---|---|
| 1 tablespoon butter | 2 teaspoons salt |
| 1 tablespoon flour | ¼ teaspoon pepper |
| 1 cup milk | 2 cups hot cooked macaroni |
| 1 cup grated cheese | 4 eggs |

Melt butter, stir in flour smoothly, and gradually add milk. Cook five minutes, stirring until smooth. Add cheese and seasonings, and cook until cheese is melted. Put macaroni in a buttered baking dish and cover with cheese sauce. Make four depressions with a spoon in the mixture, and drop an egg in each hollow. Bake fifteen minutes in a moderate oven (350 degrees F.). Serves four.

## MACARONI, SPAGHETTI, NOODLES, AND RICE IN CASSEROLE MENUS

Grapefruit Juice Cocktail
Macaroni and Haddie Casserole
Buttered Spinach      Bread and Butter
Chocolate Ice Cream and Brownies
Coffee or Tea

❋

Macaroni Neapolitan
Buttered Zucchini
Dark Rye Bread and Butter
Royal Salad
Marble Cake
Coffee

❋

Grapefruit Starter Salad
Baked Rice
Buttered Asparagus
Whole Wheat Rolls and Butter
Baked Chocolate Custard
Coffee or Tea

❋

Mexican Olla Podrida
Buttered Toasted Rolls
Tossed Green Salad
Banana Betty with Top Milk or Cream
Coffee

*Tamale Pie*
*Eggplant Casserole*
*Garden Salad*
*Whole Wheat Rolls and Butter*
*Apricot Ice Cream*
*Coffee*

❊

*Spoon Bread*
*Buttered Peas*
*Tomatoes stuffed with Mushrooms*
*Berry Loaf and Cream*
*Coffee*

## MACARONI AND HADDIE CASSEROLE

2 cups boiled macaroni
2 cups flaked finnan haddie
1 pimiento, cut in strips

1 cup grated cheese
1 cup Medium White Sauce
2 tablespoons butter

Cover bottom of buttered casserole with boiled macaroni. Spread over this a layer of the finnan haddie (which has been simmered in hot water twenty-five minutes and flaked). Add strips of pimiento, another layer of macaroni, grated cheese, a layer of fish, and pimiento. Pour the White Sauce over all. Dot with butter. Bake in a moderate oven (275 degrees F.) for twenty minutes. Serves six.

## MEXICAN OLLA PODRIDA

3 cups boiled unpolished rice
1½ cups fried onions
¾ cup grated American cheese
¼ cup butter

½ cup pimientos, chopped fine
2 cups seasoned stewed tomatoes

Rice-Cheese Soufflé, its handsome appearance enhanced by the good looking colored earthenware casserole set in which it is served.

Egg Casserole in a shallow glass baking dish, set on its own tray for serving is enhanced by a border of browned, buttered crumbs and cheese.

Cover the bottom of a well-buttered casserole with rice. Sprinkle on a layer of fried onions, then a layer of cheese, pimientos, and tomatoes. Dot with butter, and continue until all is used, making the last layer of rice and cheese. Bake covered for one hour in a moderate oven (350 degrees F.), removing the cover the last fifteen minutes to brown the top. Serves six.

## MACARONI MOUSSE

1 cup cooked macaroni
1½ cups hot milk
1 cup soft bread crumbs
¼ cup melted butter
1 pimiento, chopped fine
1 tablespoon chopped onion
1 tablespoon chopped parsley

1 cup American cheese, cut fine
¼ teaspoon salt
⅛ teaspoon pepper
3 eggs, yolks and whites separately beaten, the whites stiff

Combine milk, crumbs, butter, pimiento, onion, parsley, grated cheese, and seasonings. Then add beaten yolks and whites of eggs. Put macaroni in a buttered casserole, and pour milk and cheese mixture over it. Set in pan of hot water and bake in a slow oven (250 degrees F.) for fifty minutes, until loaf is firm. Serve with mushroom sauce. Serves six.

## MACARONI NEAPOLITAN

1 nine-ounce package elbow
   macaroni
3 tablespoons butter
3¼ tablespoons flour
2 cups milk

Salt and pepper
1½ cups grated American
   cheese
1 cup drained canned or cooked
   tomatoes

Cook the macaroni in boiling salted water until tender. Drain. Melt the butter in a double boiler, add flour, and mix well. Add milk gradually, and cook, stirring constantly until thickened.

Season with salt and pepper, and stir in the cheese. Add macaroni and tomato, and reheat in a casserole. If desired, serve with additional grated cheese. (The leftover tomato juice may be used for soup.) Six servings.

Spaghetti may be used in this recipe.

## MACARONI SOUFFLÉ

1 cup cooked elbow macaroni
1½ cups scalded milk
1 cup soft bread crumbs
¼ cup butter
¼ cup chopped pimiento

½ cup grated cheese
1 teaspoon salt
1 small onion, chopped
3 eggs, yolks and whites beaten
    separately, whites stiff

Boil macaroni until tender. Pour milk over the bread crumbs and then add butter, pimiento, cheese, salt, onion, and beaten yolks; mix and add beaten whites of eggs. Add macaroni. Pour into greased baking dish, set in a pan of hot water and bake in a slow oven (250 degrees F.) for one hour. Serves six.

## CEREAL CHEESE CASSEROLE

½ cup fine whole grain cereal
2 tablespoons butter
3 tablespoons flour

1½ cups milk
½ teaspoon salt
Few grains pepper

1 cup grated American cheese

Cook the cereal according to the directions on the package. Pour into a loaf pan and allow to cool. When firm, cut in six portions and place in a buttered shallow baking dish. Melt the butter in a double boiler, add the flour, and mix well. Add the milk gradually, and cook, stirring constantly until thickened. Add the salt and pepper. Pour the sauce over the cereal, and cover with the grated cheese. Bake in a moderate oven (350 degrees F.) for about twenty-five minutes, or until the cheese is melted and the mixture is heated through. Six servings.

## BAKED RICE

1 cup boiled rice
½ cup chopped American
    cheese
½ cup chopped pimientos
1 tablespoon sugar

1 teaspoon salt
2 eggs
1 pint milk
1 teaspoon butter
Paprika

Mix the rice with the cheese, pimientos, and seasoning. Place in a buttered casserole. Beat eggs, add milk and butter, and pour over the rice. Sprinkle with bread crumbs, and dot with butter. Bake in a moderate oven (375 degrees F.) for twenty-five minutes. Serves four.

## TAMALE PIE

3 cups milk
½ cup corn meal
2 teaspoons salt
2 tablespoons chopped green
    pepper

2 tablespoons minced onion
1 pound ground beef
3 tablespoons butter
Few grains pepper
2½ tablespoons flour

1 cup drained cooked tomatoes

Put two cups of the milk in a double boiler, add corn meal and one-half teaspoon of the salt, and cook, stirring constantly until thickened. Pour into a buttered baking dish; when slightly cool, spread the mixture against the sides and bottom so that the dish is lined with the mush.

Fry the green pepper, onion, and beef in the butter, and add pepper and the remaining one and one-half teaspoons salt. Stir in the flour and add the remaining one cup of milk. Cook, stirring constantly until thickened. Add tomatoes and pour into the baking dish. Bake in a hot oven (400 degrees F.) for twenty to thirty minutes. Six servings.

## SPAGHETTI AND TOMATO CASSEROLE

2 slices diced raw bacon
1 tablespoon minced onion
1 chicken liver
2 tablespoons diced mush-
    rooms, fresh or canned

½ teaspoon paprika
1½ cups canned tomatoes
½ package spaghetti
Salt and pepper
2 tablespoons buttered crumbs

1 tablespoon grated cheese

Cook bacon for a few minutes in a hot pan, then add onion and chicken liver, and cook five minutes. Drain off any excess fat, add mushrooms, paprika, and tomatoes, and let simmer for twenty minutes. Cook spaghetti until tender in boiling water. Drain, combine with the first mixture, season, and turn into the casserole; top with crumbs into which cheese has been stirred. Bake in a moderate oven (375 degrees F.) about ten minutes. Serves four to five.

In nearly all recipes calling for noodles or macaroni, spaghetti may be substituted, and the other way round too.

## RICE-CHEESE SOUFFLÉ

2 tablespoons butter or mar-
    garine
3 tablespoons flour
¾ cup milk

½ pound American cheese,
    shredded
1 cup cooked rice
4 eggs

Salt and pepper

Make a sauce with the butter or margarine, flour and milk. Add the shredded cheese and stir until it is all melted. Add the rice and beaten egg yolks, with seasonings to taste. Fold in stiffly beaten egg whites. Bake in a moderate oven (315 degrees F.) one hour or until firm. Serves four to six.

## RICE AND OKRA CASSEROLE

1 cup cooked rice
½ pound okra
⅓ cup butter

1 minced onion
1 tablespoon curry powder
4 cups stewed tomatoes

Fry onion in butter. Cut okra in small pieces crosswise, and combine with all other ingredients. Season with salt and pepper. Put in a buttered casserole and bake in a slow oven (250 degrees F.) for two hours. Serves six.

## SPOON BREAD

1 cup white or yellow corn
    meal
1 cup milk
1 teaspoon salt

1 tablespoon butter, melted
1 cup boiling water
2 teaspoons sugar
2 whole eggs

1 teaspoon baking powder

Stir corn meal and butter into the boiling water smoothly. Let cool. When the mixture is cold, add the salt, sugar, and eggs, and beat well until mixed. Stir in the milk, mix well, and stir in the baking powder. Pour into a buttered baking dish and bake twenty minutes in a moderate oven (375 degrees F.), until the spoon bread has risen and is a light golden brown. Serves four.

# CHICKEN CASSEROLE DINNERS

Brunswick Stew
Hot Biscuits and Butter with Peach Jam
Asparagus Vinaigrette
Chocolate Custard Pie
Coffee or Tea

❋

Chicken and Ham Van Loon
Baked Potatoes     Buttered Spinach
French Rolls and Butter with Black Currant Jam
Strawberry-Raspberry Dessert
Coffee

❋

Tomato Juice Cocktail
Chicken and Noodles
Italian Whole Rye Bread and Butter
Stuffed Baked Onions
Romaine and Grapefruit Salad
Cake and Coffee

❋

Tomato Bisque
Chicken in Sauerkraut
Baked Lima Beans
Pumpernickel and Butter
Raisin Cake
Coffee

*Chicken Soufflé*
*Baked Potatoes      Asparagus with Cheese*
*Melba Toast and Butter*
*Cherries Morocco on Vanilla Ice Cream*
*Coffee*

❊

*Farmer's Chicken Pie*
*Scalloped Potatoes*
*Stewed Tomatoes*
*Biscuits and Butter with Peach Jam*
*Apple Custard*
*Coffee*

❊

*Potted Roasting Chicken with Vegetables*
*Tossed Green Salad      Cottage Cheese*
*Toasted Rolls and Butter*
*Southern Soufflé*
*Coffee*

❊

*Smothered Chicken*
*Cauliflower au Gratin*
*Peas Breton*
*Raisin Bread and Butter*
*Orange Sherbet and Cookies*
*Coffee or Tea*

*Smothered Chicken*
*Eggplant with Cheese and Tomatoes*
*Rolls and Butter*
*Filled Pineapple and Cookies*
*Coffee or Tea*

*

*Broiled Grapefruit with Honey*
*Spanish Turkey*
*Buttered Carrots*
*Tossed Green Salad*
*Swedish Bread and Butter*
*Chocolate Icebox Cake*
*Coffee*

## BAKED CHICKEN

2 frying chickens (2 to 2½     Salt and pepper
    pounds each)     Butter
Flour     3 cups milk

Cut the chicken into serving pieces. Dip in flour well seasoned with salt and pepper. Fry in butter over low heat, turning until brown on all sides, keeping the pan covered as much as possible. Place the chicken in a deep casserole and cover with scalded milk. Cover tightly and bake in a slow oven (300 degrees F.) for thirty to thirty-five minutes, or until tender. Remove chicken and keep it hot. Make gravy in a pan using three and one-half tablespoons of flour and a little water to make a paste, and add the milk and broth from the casserole. Cook, stirring constantly until thickened. Season with salt and pepper, and pour over the chicken which has been put back in the casserole. Reheat a few minutes. Serves six to eight.

## BRUNSWICK STEW

2 chickens
2 gallons cold water
6 potatoes
3 hard-cooked eggs
1 quart sweet corn cut from the cob or canned, or quick-frozen (2 packages)

1 quart tomatoes
12 crackers
2 tablespoons Worcestershire Sauce
½ cup butter
Salt and pepper

Boil chickens in water until they are tender enough to bone. Wash and peel potatoes, and let stand in cold water one and one-half hours. Remove chickens from the kettle, skin and bone them. Put corn, peeled and cut tomatoes, and chopped potatoes into a deep casserole and cover with the broth from the kettle. Cook until the potatoes are almost tender, then add the chicken meat diced or left in good-sized pieces, as you prefer. Cook in a hot oven (425 degrees F.) for one-half hour. Chop two of the eggs fine, and slice the other. Add with the remaining ingredients to the stew. Serves eight to ten.

## CHICKEN AND HAM VAN LOON

7 slices white meat of cooked chicken, cut in uniform size
3 slices boiled ham, cut same size
½ small Bermuda onion, finely minced
¼ cup butter

½ cup sliced mushrooms
1 teaspoon paprika
1 teaspoon salt
¼ teaspoon grated nutmeg
¾ cup cream
3 to 4 tablespoons Parmesan cheese, grated

Cook the minced onion in the butter for five minutes, stirring constantly, and do not let it brown. Add the sliced mushrooms and seasonings, and let simmer for fifteen minutes. Then turn the mixture into an oblong baking dish, and arrange chicken and ham on the top. Add enough hot cream to cover the meat; let simmer in a hot oven (400 degrees F.) for ten minutes. Then cover with Parmesan cheese; let remain in the oven until the cheese is browned. Serves six.

## CHICKEN AND NOODLES

¼ cup butter
2 tablespoons minced green
    pepper
1 cup sliced mushrooms
¼ cup chopped pimiento
1½ tablespoons flour

2 cups cooked noodles
2 cups thin cream
2 cups chopped chicken
1 teaspoon salt
⅛ teaspoon pepper
2 egg yolks, beaten

Grated Parmesan cheese

Simmer green pepper in butter until tender; then add mushrooms and pimiento. Blend in flour, gradually add cream, and cook ten minutes, stirring constantly. Add chicken and seasonings, and cook three minutes. Pour noodles in the bottom of a casserole, top with the chicken mixture to which the egg yolks have been added. Sprinkle with cheese. Set in a hot oven (425 degrees F.) ten minutes. Serves six.

## CHICKEN IN SAUERKRAUT

1 small roasting chicken,
    dressed and cleaned
1½ cups mashed potatoes

8 slices bacon
2 cups sauerkraut
Flour

Seasonings

Stuff the seasoned chicken with the mashed potatoes, and cover with a paste of flour and water. Place four slices of bacon in the bottom of a deep casserole, then a layer of kraut; lay the chicken on this, cover with kraut, and arrange the remaining slices of bacon on top. Pour very little water around the chicken to moisten the kraut. Set in a moderate oven (325 degrees F.) and bake three hours. Watch, and if it seems too dry, add a few spoonfuls of hot water. For easier service, some prefer to cut the chicken into serving pieces first. Six servings.

## CHICKEN PIE

| | |
|---|---|
| 1 chicken | ¼ cup sherry |
| 2 tablespoons fat | *For the pastry use:* |
| 1 large onion | 2 cups flour |
| 2 large tomatoes | ¼ cup sugar |
| ¼ cup each ripe olives, seedless | ¼ cup butter |
|    raisins, almonds | 1 cup lard |
|    shredded | 1 egg |
| Salt and pepper | ½ teaspoon salt |

Boil the chicken until tender; drain, and cut the meat from the bones. Put two tablespoons of fat in a frying pan, brown the onion sliced very fine, then add the tomatoes cut in small pieces. Add raisins, olives, and almonds. Cook for ten minutes; add the chicken and seasoning, and cook ten minutes longer, adding sherry at the last minute.

Roll out the pastry about one-fourth-inch thick; line the bottom and sides of the casserole with the paste; put in the mixture and cover with pierced pastry top. Bake forty minutes in a hot oven (400 degrees F.), until the pastry is nicely browned. Serves six.

## SMOTHERED CHICKEN

| | |
|---|---|
| 3 small broiling chickens (2½ | ½ pound butter |
|    pounds) | ½ cup flour |
| 3 giblets | 2 cups cream |
| 3 cups stock | Salt and pepper |

Split the cleaned and dressed chickens down the back, and season. Roll in flour. Heat butter in a frying pan and brown the chickens on all sides. Place in a casserole, breast side down, with the giblets under them. Add the broth, cover the casserole closely, and cook for one and one-half hours, basting every ten to fifteen minutes. When done, remove the chickens and keep hot. Mash the giblets and add cream to the casserole, stirring until smooth. Heat thoroughly, then lay the chickens back in the casserole, basting the sauce over all pieces. Serves six.

## CHICKEN SOUFFLÉ I

3 tablespoons butter
3 tablespoons flour
¼ teaspoon salt
⅛ teaspoon pepper

1 cup thin cream
3 eggs, separated
1 cup cooked chicken
1 tablespoon finely chopped parsley

Melt butter in the double boiler, add flour and seasoning, stirring smoothly. Gradually stir in milk. Cook until sauce thickens. Add finely chopped chicken and beaten egg yolks. Cook one minute longer. Remove from heat and let cool slightly. Fold in stiffly beaten egg whites. Turn into buttered baking dish, set in a pan of hot water, and bake in moderate oven (350 degrees F.) forty-five minutes. Serves four.

## CHICKEN SOUFFLÉ II

1 cup chicken, minced or put twice through food chopper
3 eggs
1 tablespoon butter

1 tablespoon flour
1 tablespoon minced onion
1 tablespoon minced parsley
1 cup milk or cream
½ teaspoon salt

Paprika

Make a white sauce of the butter, flour, milk, and salt. Remove from the heat, and add the beaten yolks of eggs and the chicken. Return to the fire and cook a few seconds but do not boil. Let cool. Twenty minutes before serving, add stiffly beaten egg whites to the mixture and beat together. Put in a well-buttered casserole, set in a pan of hot water, and bake in a moderate oven (350 degrees F.) about twenty minutes. Serves four.

## FARMER'S CHICKEN PIE

3 carrots
1 onion, minced
½ cup chicken broth
1 cup cooked green peas
2 cups cooked chicken, diced
Salt and pepper

1½ tablespoons flour
½ cup milk
1 small can mushrooms
 (optional)
5 slices dry white bread
Swiss cheese, sliced

Cut carrots in strips and cook in boiling salted water for seven minutes. Pour off water except enough to cover the carrots, add onions and boil ten minutes. Add chicken broth, peas, chicken, and seasonings. Simmer fifteen minutes. Add milk and flour, and blend in smoothly; then add mushrooms and one-third their juice. Simmer several minutes, then pour into a casserole. Cut bread in squares, toast on one side, and place toasted side down to make a top for the pie. Cover the untoasted side of the bread with cheese and set the casserole in a moderate oven (375 degrees F.) until the cheese melts. Serves six.

## SPANISH TURKEY

1 cup cooked turkey, minced
¼ cup minced ham
1 cup mashed potatoes
½ cup turkey gravy
Salt and pepper

2 cups hot boiled rice
1 finely minced clove garlic
3 canned pimientos, chopped
 fine
¼ cup grated cheese

Mix meats and potatoes with gravy, and season to taste. Put into a buttered shallow baking dish and cover with a layer of rice into which the garlic and pimientos have been stirred. Sprinkle with cheese and heat in a hot oven (425 degrees F.) till the cheese has melted and begins to brown. Serves four to six.

## POTTED ROASTING CHICKEN WITH VEGETABLES

| | |
|---|---|
| 1 roasting chicken | 1 cup green peas |
| Giblets | 1 cup diced green beans |
| 8 small onions, peeled | 1 cup sliced mushrooms |
| 8 small new potatoes | 1 cup water |
| 8 small carrots | 1½ teaspoons salt |

Crumb stuffing

Use a simple well-seasoned bread stuffing. Tie the legs of the chicken together, just as you would for the roasting pan. Put the chicken, breast side up, and the giblets in a three-quart casserole. Bake uncovered in a hot oven (425 degrees F.) fifteen minutes. Remove the liver, and reduce the heat to moderate (325 degrees F.). Add the onions, cover and bake half an hour. Then add the potatoes and carrots, scrubbed but not peeled. Add the one cup of water; cover and let cook one-half hour. Add peas, beans, and mushrooms. Sprinkle with salt, and bake covered for another half hour. When serving, slip the chicken meat from the bones and transfer it to a hot platter. Place spoonfuls of the hot vegetables around it. Serves six.

# MEAT CASSEROLE DINNERS

Pineapple Mint Cup
Beef Biscuit Roll and Gravy
Carrots and Peas
Bread and Butter
Orange Bavarian
Coffee or Tea

❋

Beef Casserole Supper
Rye Bread and Butter with Jam
Grapefruit Perfection Salad
Marvel Chocolate Pie
Coffee

❋

Beef Miroton
Scalloped Sweet Potatoes and Apple
Tossed Green Salad      Cottage Cheese
French Bread and Butter
New Orleans Fudge Loaf
Coffee

❋

Vegetable Juice Cocktail
Bologna with Noodles or Macaroni
Whole Wheat Crackers and Butter
Garden Salad
Honeydew Melon
Coffee

*Cream of Celery Soup with Cheese Crackers*
*Heart Pie*
*Raw Vegetable Salad*
*Corn Sticks and Butter*
*Apple Pie*
*Coffee*

❋

*Ham and Veal in Casserole*
*Tossed Green Salad*
*Toasted Whole Wheat Rolls and Butter*
*Rice Custard Brazilian*
*Coffee*

❋

*Chilled Mixed Fruit Juices*
*Pork Tenderloin Creole*
*Potatoes boiled in Jackets*
*Melba Toast and Butter*
*Chocolate Peppermint Cake*
*Coffee or Tea*

❋

*Jellied Tomato Bouillon*
*Sausage with Sweet Potato Topping*
*Buttered Asparagus*
*Hot Popovers and Butter*
*Apple Delicious*
*Coffee or Tea*

Baked Chicken in a large, oval casserole, one of the most popular recipes for year-round cookery.

**Liver and Eggplant Casserole** ready for the oven. This two-handled, bright-colored baking dish is popular for many types of oven cookery.

*Tomato Soup with Whole Wheat Crackers*
*Lamb with Lima Beans*
*Western Fruit Plate*
*Devil's Food Cake*
*Coffee*

✿

*Braised Calf's Liver*
*Hot Cheese Biscuits and Butter*
*Artichoke Hearts and Tomato Salad*
*Berry Loaf and Cream*
*Coffee*

✿

*Melon*
*Liver and Vegetable Pie*
*Pumpernickel and Butter*
*Royal Salad      Cottage Cheese*
*Coffee or Tea*

✿

*Sweetbreads in Casserole*
*Chef's California Salad Bowl*
*Toasted Rolls and Butter*
*Chocolate Soufflé*
*Coffee*

✿

*Appetizer Tray of Carrot Sticks, Celery, Olives, Radishes*
*Veal Potpie*
*Whole Wheat Bread and Butter*
*Swedish Apple Pudding*
*Coffee or Tea*

*Cream of Asparagus Soup with Celery Crackers*
*Tongue and Peas Scalloped*
*Oatmeal Bread and Butter*
*Orange Sherbet and Cookies*
*Coffee or Tea*

✿

*Grapefruit Starter Salad*
*Shepherd's Pie*
*Protein Bread and Butter*
*Coconut Bread Pudding with Sauce*
*Coffee or Tea*

## BEEF BISCUIT ROLL

1 pound ground beef chuck
½ cup chopped onion
¼ cup chopped green pepper

½ teaspoon salt
⅛ teaspoon pepper
Butter or beef fat

Brown the onion, green pepper, and beef in butter or beef fat in a frying pan. Add the seasonings. Make a regulation biscuit dough; spread dough with meat mixture and roll like jelly roll. If dough is too soft, chill in refrigerator first; cut the roll in one-and-one-half-inch slices. Place in greased pan, cut side up, brush tops with melted butter. Bake twenty to twenty-five minutes in a hot oven (450 degrees F.). Serve with brown gravy or cheese sauce. Makes five or six servings.

## BEEF MIROTON

1 pound cooked beef
2 small onions
2 tablespoons butter
1 tablespoon flour

1 cup stock (or use bouillon cubes)
Bread crumbs
Salt and pepper

Cut the beef thin and remove any gristle. Chop the onions fine, and brown in the butter. Add the flour and brown it, then the stock, stirring to make a thin gravy. Add salt and pepper, and pour over the beef slices which have been laid in a casserole. Sprinkle with bread crumbs and set in a moderate oven (375 degrees F.) about thirty minutes. Four to five servings.

## BEEF CASSEROLE SUPPER

2 pounds beef chuck
2 teaspoons salt
½ teaspoon white pepper
1 tablespoon flour
1 large Spanish onion
3 tablespoons butter

6 medium potatoes
1⅓ cups boiling water
½ teaspoon meat extract, or moistened bouillon cube
3 to 4 tablespoons white wine, sherry, or beer (this is optional)

Cut beef into small pieces easily served. Sprinkle with a mixture of salt, pepper, and flour. Peel and slice the onion, and fry till yellow in half of the butter. Peel potatoes and cut into slices about one-fourth-inch thick. Butter a casserole and fill with potatoes, meat, and onions in separate layers, seasoning the potato layers with salt. Pour over this the water mixed with the meat extract and the wine. Simmer covered in a moderate oven (325 degrees F.) about two hours until the meat is tender. Serves six.

## BEEF PIE

1½ pounds cold roast beef, cut in thin slices
Flour, salt, and pepper

2 cups minced onion
1 cup gravy or bouillon
2 cups mashed potatoes

1 egg, beaten

Put thin slices of cold roast beef on the bottom of a casserole. Dredge with a little flour, pepper, and salt. Add a layer of minced onion, then another layer of beef and seasoning, and repeat until the dish is filled. Pour on any leftover beef gravy, or one cup of bouillon made with bouillon cubes. Boil and mash potatoes, add milk, butter, and salt to them beating well, then spread one inch thick on top of the pie. Brush the top with beaten egg, set in a hot oven (425 degrees F.), and bake till the potato is browned. Serves four.

## BEEF PIE CAVANAGH

3 pounds beef, cut in cubes
12 small whole onions
4 carrots, diced
¼ pound mushrooms, sliced
1 teaspoon black pepper,
     freshly ground
Rich pastry

1 cup stock or bouillon
1 sprig tarragon
1 sprig thyme
1 sprig sage
½ bay leaf
¾ cup red wine
Butter

Melt the butter in the casserole and heat the beef cubes in it until slightly browned and cooked through. Add stock or one cup of water, and simmer slowly for one hour. Add onions, carrots, mushrooms, seasonings, and herbs. Simmer for one-half hour more. Remove herbs. Add wine and cover with rich pastry crust. Bake in a hot oven (400 degrees F.) fifteen to twenty minutes, till crust is brown. Serves six.

## BEEFSTEAK AND KIDNEY PIE

1 pound beef chuck or round
     steak
1 veal kidney
½ large onion
1 tablespoon lard or butter

1½ teaspoons salt
⅛ teaspoon pepper
½ tablespoon Worcestershire
     Sauce
1 tablespoon flour

½ cup boiling water

Soak kidney in cold salted water for thirty minutes. Cut meat in one-inch cubes. Drain kidney and cut into even smaller cubes. Let sliced onion brown slowly in lard or butter, then add meats and brown well on all sides. Add salt, pepper, Worcestershire Sauce, and the half cup of boiling water. Simmer slowly for two hours or until very tender. Mix the flour with one-quarter cup cold water, and stir into the meat to thicken it. Transfer to baking dish or individual casseroles and cover top with thin pastry with hole in center for escape of steam. Bake thirty minutes in a moderate oven (375 degrees F.). Serves four.

## BOLOGNA WITH NOODLES OR MACARONI

1 cup bologna, cut in small
    pieces
3 cups hot cooked noodles or
    macaroni
½ teaspoon salt and pepper
    mixed

½ cup milk
½ cup water
½ cup cracker or bread crumbs
1 tablespoon butter

Grease a baking dish, place in it alternate layers of chopped bologna and cooked noodles or macaroni. Season with salt and pepper. Add liquid, cover with bread crumbs, dot with butter, and brown in a hot oven (400 degrees F.). Serves six.

## CHILI CON CARNE EN CASSEROLE

2 fresh or dried chili peppers
2 pounds round steak
¼ cup drippings, butter, or lard

4 tablespoons flour
1 clove garlic
1 teaspoon salt
1 cup dried beans

Soak the beans overnight, drain and let simmer until tender. Discard the seeds in the peppers; if dried peppers are used, soak them in warm water to cover until soft; scrape the pulp into the water and discard the skin. Save the pulp and water.

Cut the steak in small pieces, and cook in the melted fat in a frying pan until well browned. Place in a casserole. Add the flour to the fat left in the pan and stir until browned. Add the chili paste and water, and stir until boiling, then the cut clove of garlic; then add to the meat in the casserole. Cover and simmer until the meat is tender (350 degrees F.) about two hours, adding hot water as needed. When the meat is tender the sauce should be of good consistency. Add the salt. The beans should be tender and most of the water evaporated. Season with salt and pepper and a little butter, mix well and add to the meat in the casserole. Let heat thoroughly together. Serves six to eight.

## HAM AND VEAL EN CASSEROLE

¾ pound veal
3 tablespoons butter
¼ pound ham
6 small onions
1 cup tomatoes
1 cup stock
Pepper

2 cups potatoes, cut in cubes
　or balls
3 tablespoons flour
1 cup string beans, cooked
½ cup celery, minced
2 tablespoons sugar
1 teaspoon salt

Cut the veal and ham in small pieces and toss until browned slightly in one tablespoon of the butter or fat. Place in a casserole. Brown the onions in the rest of the butter and two tablespoons of sugar; add to the meat with the stock, seasonings, tomatoes, and celery. Cover and cook in a moderate oven (325 degrees F.) one hour. Then add the potatoes and cook until they are soft. Thicken the gravy by stirring in a very little flour rubbed smooth in cold water. Add the string beans, cover and let simmer for ten minutes longer. Serves six.

## HEART PIE

| | |
|---|---|
| 1 pound heart (beef, lamb, veal, or pork) | 2 tablespoons butter |
| | 2 cups hot water |
| Salt and pepper | 1 cup milk |
| Flour | Fluffy mashed potatoes |

Wash the heart, cut away any tough tubes and remove excess fat. Cut in small cubes, sprinkle with salt and pepper, and roll in flour. Fry in butter until brown on all sides. Add the hot water, cover and cook over low heat for one and a half to two hours, or until tender. Add more water, if necessary, to keep it from burning. Mix two tablespoons of flour with a little of the milk until smooth. Add remaining milk and stir into heart mixture. Cook over low heat, stirring constantly until thickened. Season with salt and pepper. Pour into casserole and cover with mashed potatoes. Brown in a hot oven (400 degrees F.) about twenty-five minutes. Six servings.

## SCALLOPED HAM

| | |
|---|---|
| 4 cups cold cooked ham, minced | 1 teaspoon French mustard |
| | 1 teaspoon paprika |
| 2 cups bread crumbs | 3 tablespoons melted butter |
| 8 hard-cooked eggs, chopped | 1 quart milk |

Mix all ingredients, adding milk last. Turn into a buttered casserole; sprinkle the top lightly with a few buttered crumbs, and bake in a moderate oven (300 degrees F.) one hour. Serves eight.

## HAM WITH SCALLOPED POTATOES

| | |
|---|---|
| Raw potatoes, pared and sliced | Flour |
| 1 slice ham for broiling | ¾ to 1 cup milk |
| Pepper and salt | 1 clove garlic |

Rub a buttered baking dish with a cut clove of garlic. Fill the dish three-quarters full of pared, sliced raw potatoes sprinkled generously with flour. Season with salt and pepper, and pour milk over all. Lay the slice of ham over this. Bake in a moderate oven (375 degrees F.) forty-five minutes. The ham should be tender and browned. Serves six.

## LAMB NECK SLICES

| | |
|---|---|
| 2 pounds lamb neck slices | ⅛ teaspoon pepper |
| 2 tablespoons lard | 3 medium onions, peeled |
| 1 cup water | 3 potatoes, pared |
| 1 teaspoon salt | 6 small carrots, pared |
| 6 large stalks celery | |

Brown neck slices in hot lard in a frying pan. Then turn into a casserole and add water and seasonings. Cover and allow to simmer for one hour. Add onions and lengthwise strips of carrots and potatoes. Continue to simmer twenty minutes. Then add celery, cut in three-inch pieces, and simmer fifteen minutes longer. Serves six.

## LAMB WITH LIMA BEANS

| | |
|---|---|
| 1½ pounds lamb shoulder | 1 small onion or clove of gar- |
| ¼ pound dried Lima beans | lic, chopped |
| 2 tablespoons bacon drippings | 1½ teaspoons salt |
|    or lard | ⅛ teaspoon pepper |
| 1 cup boiling water | |

Wash Lima beans and soak overnight in cold water. Drain. Cut lamb into one-inch pieces and brown in the fat with the onion or garlic. Add salt and pepper, and place in casserole. Add Lima beans and boiling water; cover and cook in slow oven (300 degrees F.) about one hour, or until both meat and beans are tender. Serves five or six.

# BRAISED CALF'S LIVER

1½ pounds calf's liver  
6 slices bacon  
2 teaspoons chopped parsley  
½ cup sliced carrots  

1 tablespoon olive oil  
3 onions, thinly sliced  
¾ cup stock, or use bouillon  
        cube  

Salt and pepper

Cut the liver into slices a little less than one-half-inch thick. Cover with boiling water and let stand five minutes to draw out some of the blood. Drain and remove veins and outside membrane. Rub the bottom of a casserole with olive oil. Lay in the sliced liver. On this sprinkle the onions, carrots, and parsley. Put in the rest of the liver and top with the sliced bacon. Pour in the stock. Cover and cook in a slow oven (275 degrees F.) until the meat is tender. Remove the cover and set under the broiler a few minutes. Add a few tablespoons of white wine with the stock if you like. Serves six.

# LIVER EGGPLANT CASSEROLE

1 medium eggplant  
1¼ pounds sliced beef liver  
Butter  
Salt and pepper  

3 tablespoons flour  
1¼ cups milk  
3 tablespoons catsup  
Buttered soft bread crumbs  

Pare eggplant and cut in cubes. Cook in a very small quantity of boiling salted water until tender. Drain, and boil down the liquid to one-quarter cup. Place the eggplant in a buttered baking dish.

Fry the liver in butter until browned on both sides and partially cooked. Cut in small cubes, place on the eggplant, and sprinkle with salt and pepper. Add the flour to the drippings in the frying pan and mix well. (Add more butter if necessary.) Add the milk gradually and cook, stirring constantly until thickened. Add the eggplant liquid and catsup, and stir until well mixed. Season with salt and pepper, and pour over the liver. Cover with the crumbs, and bake in a moderately hot oven (375 degrees F.) about twenty-five minutes, or until the liver is completely cooked and the crumbs are browned. Serves six.

## LIVER AND VEGETABLE PIE

3 slices bacon
1 pound liver, cut in small
    pieces
1½ cups sliced onions
1 cup chopped celery
2 tablespoons chopped celery
    leaves
1 cup diced carrots
1 beef bouillon cube
2 teaspoons salt
3 cups boiling water

Dash of sage
⅛ teaspoon paprika
Dash of pepper
½ teaspoon Worcestershire
    Sauce
1½ cups sifted flour
1½ teaspoons baking powder
¼ teaspoon salt
5 tablespoons butter or other
    shortening
½ cup milk (about)

Fry bacon; add liver and onions and brown slightly. Add celery, celery leaves, carrots, bouillon cube, and salt to boiling water, and cook until celery and carrots are tender. Drain; measure liquid and add water to make two cups. Add meat mixture and vegetables to liquid; then add remaining ingredients and bring to boiling and boil briskly, stirring constantly. Turn into a greased shallow casserole.

Sift flour once, measure, add baking powder and salt, and sift again. Cut in shortening. Add milk all at once, and stir carefully until all flour is dampened. Then stir vigorously until mixture forms a soft dough and follows spoon around the bowl. Turn out on lightly floured board and knead thirty seconds. Roll dough one-fourth inch thick; with sharp knife make slits to permit escape of steam. Fit over meat mixture in casserole. Bake in a hot oven (450 degrees F.) twenty minutes, or until crust is browned. Serves six to eight.

## SCALLOPED LIVER AND POTATOES

1 pound calf's liver
Seasoned flour
3 tablespoons lard
3½ cups thinly sliced potatoes
3 tablespoons butter

3 tablespoons flour
1½ cups milk
Salt and pepper
Soft bread crumbs
1 cup sliced onions

Dredge liver in flour; brown in two tablespoons lard. Cube liver. Pan-fry potatoes and onions in the remaining lard until brown and tender. Melt butter; blend in flour. Add milk; cook, stirring constantly until thickened. Season. Arrange liver, potatoes, onions, and sauce in layers in a casserole. Top with crumbs. Bake in a moderate oven (350 degrees F.) twenty minutes. Serves four.

## PORK TENDERLOIN BAKED IN CREAM

Pork tenderloin, cut crosswise
    in 2-inch pieces
Salt and pepper

Flour
2 tablespoons lard or bacon
    drippings
½ cup light cream or top milk

Place each slice of pork tenderloin between pieces of waxed paper and flatten with wooden potato masher or mallet. Season with salt and pepper; sprinkle with flour, fry in lard or bacon drippings until well browned. Place in baking dish. Add one-half cup light cream or top milk to the drippings in pan, bring to a boil and pour over meat. Cover and simmer, or bake in moderate oven (350 degrees F.) about one-half hour, or until tender. One large tenderloin will provide six pieces. Allow one to two pieces per portion.

## PORK TENDERLOIN CREOLE

1½ pounds pork tenderloin,     2 cups tomatoes
    sliced                          1 teaspoon salt
3 tablespoons flour            4 carrots
3 tablespoons lard             1 onion, sliced
        ½ green pepper, diced

Dredge meat with flour; brown in lard. Pour tomatoes over meat, add seasonings, onion, carrots, and green pepper. Place in covered casserole, and cook in slow oven (300 degrees F.) one hour. Serves four.

## POT ROAST IN A CASSEROLE

4 pounds beef                  ½ cup rum or sherry
3 tablespoons butter           1 cup green olives
Salt and pepper                2 tablespoons tomato paste

Season meat with salt and pepper and fry in butter in a frying pan until brown. Put in a deep casserole and pour over it the rum or sherry. Cook one-half hour in a moderate oven (375 degrees F.), then add tomato paste and let simmer slowly three more hours in a low oven (275 to 300 degrees F.). Add stoned olives a few minutes before serving, just long enough to let them heat through. Eight to ten servings.

## SHORT RIBS BARBECUED

3 pounds short ribs            ½ cup water
2 tablespoons lard             3 tablespoons Worcestershire
1 medium onion                     Sauce (optional)
¼ cup vinegar                  1 teaspoon prepared mustard
2 tablespoons brown sugar      ½ cup diced celery
1 cup catsup                   2 teaspoons salt

Have ribs cut into sections two to three inches long. Brown in lard. Brown minced onion. Add all remaining ingredients to short ribs. Cover and cook slowly, or bake in a moderate oven (350 degrees F.) one and a half to two hours, or until tender. Serves four to five.

## SAUSAGE MEAT WITH BAKED APPLES

6 large tart apples           Sugar
1 cup partly cooked sausage
    meat

Scoop out the centers of the apples, leaving a thick shell, and be careful not to pierce the bottom. Chop and mix the apple cut from the cores and part of another apple, to make one cup, with the sausage meat. Sprinkle apple centers with sugar; then stuff with the mixture, heaping it well on top. Bake in a casserole, with a few tablespoons of water in the bottom, till tender and the sausage is cooked and browned on top (375 degrees F.). Serves six.

## SWEETBREADS IN A CASSEROLE

2 pairs sweetbreads         6 small cooked onions
Salt                      1 cup cooked or canned peas
Vinegar              1 cup diced cooked potatoes
3 tablespoons butter      3 strips bacon
2 cups sliced cooked carrots  1 cup chicken bouillon

Soak sweetbreads in cold water one-half hour; remove membrane. Simmer fifteen minutes in water to which one teaspoon salt and one tablespoon vinegar have been added for each quart of water. Drain; place in cold water. Brown sweetbreads in butter; place in the baking dish. Arrange vegetables around the sweetbreads; cover with bacon. Add bouillon; cover. Bake in moderate oven (350 degrees F.) twenty minutes. Serves six.

## SAUSAGE WITH SWEET POTATO TOPPING

1 pound sausage
4 tablespoons flour

2 cups milk
Fluffy mashed sweet potatoes

Fry the sausage and drain off excess fat. Cut in pieces and return to the pan. Add the flour and mix well. Add the milk gradually and cook, stirring constantly until thickened. Add salt and pepper if desired. Pour into a buttered shallow baking dish, and pile the sweet potatoes on the top. Brown in a hot oven (400 degrees F.) or under the broiler. Six servings.

## SHEPHERD'S PIE

2 cups cooked meat, finely
    chopped
4 tablespoons chili sauce

Butter, salt, pepper
2 cups hot mashed potatoes
2 egg yolks

3 tablespoons milk

Season the meat with salt and pepper and small dabs of butter, adding the chili sauce. Put in a shallow baking dish and cover with the mashed potatoes. Brush with yolk of egg mixed with the milk. Set in a moderate oven (375 degrees F.) until lightly browned. Serves six.

## CREAMED SWEETBREADS AND MUSHROOMS

1 pound sweetbreads
1 cup chopped mushrooms,
    steamed
1 teaspoon salt
1 tablespoon vinegar

1 cup cream
1 tablespoon flour
2 tablespoons butter, melted
2 egg yolks
¼ teaspoon pepper

½ teaspoon salt

Soak sweetbreads in cold water fifteen minutes. Remove membranes and cook sweetbreads for twenty minutes in boiling water to which one teaspoon salt and one tablespoon vinegar have been added. Drain and cover with cold water to harden and whiten. Cut in cubes; add to cream sauce made by heating the cream, then adding the flour and butter creamed together, the beaten egg yolks, and seasoning, stirred together as it thickens. Place squares or triangles of buttered toast in the bottom of a shallow casserole. Cover with mushrooms and sweetbread mixture. Heat a few minutes in a hot oven (400 degrees F.). Garnish with parsley and serve. Serves six.

## TONGUE AND PEAS SCALLOPED

Cover a fresh tongue with cold water; add one-and-one-half teaspoons salt to each quart of water; bring to boiling. Simmer slowly until tender, allowing one to one and a half hours. Keep tongue in the liquid until cool enough to handle, then remove outer skin.

| | |
|---|---|
| 2 cups cooked tongue | 2 cups Medium White Sauce |
| 1 cup cooked peas | Grated cheese |

Slice tongue, then cut into small pieces. Combine with cooked peas and White Sauce. Place in buttered casserole. Top with grated cheese. Bake in a moderate oven (350 degrees F.) about thirty minutes. Serves five or six.

## TONGUE AU GRATIN

Leftover cooked tongue, cut into slices. A little chervil, parsley, shallots, tarragon and capers, chopped together very fine; and one minced and pounded anchovy added to this. Butter a baking dish, and lay the slices of tongue in it, spreading each with the herb mixture. Sprinkle bread crumbs on top. Dot with butter and salt and a little pepper. Brown in a moderate oven (375 degrees F.) fifteen to twenty minutes, or until the crumbs are browned slightly.

## BAKED CREOLE TRIPE

1 pound tripe
2 cups chopped celery
1 cup sliced onions
2 tablespoons chopped green
    pepper

3 tablespoons lard
2 cups tomato juice
¾ teaspoon salt
Dash of pepper
1 cup soft bread crumbs

Precook tripe as directed below; cut in strips one-half inch wide. Combine celery, onions, and green pepper; brown in hot lard. Put vegetables into a casserole; add tripe. Mix tomato juice, salt, and pepper; pour over the tripe. Top with crumbs. Cover; bake (350 degrees F.) two hours. Serves four to six.

*To precook tripe* for use in many dishes, first wash thoroughly in two or three cold waters; then cover with salted water and simmer until tender, one to two hours. Cook it thoroughly. (If pickled tripe is used, soak fifteen minutes in cold salted water before cooking.)

## VEAL AND HAM PIE

2 pounds raw lean ham, cut
    very thin
2 pounds raw veal cutlet, very
    thin
2 onions, chopped very fine
¼ bunch parsley, chopped fine

1 teaspoon black pepper
3 tablespoons sherry
½ cup chicken or beef broth
1 tablespoon Worcestershire
    Sauce
Rich pastry for top

On the bottom of the baking dish, place a layer of the thinly sliced raw ham. On top of this, place a layer of the veal. Sprinkle with some of the chopped onions and parsley. Season with black pepper. Use no salt. Repeat layers and seasonings until all have been used. Over all, pour the broth, and on top put a dash of the Worcestershire. Pour on the sherry. Cover the dish with rich pastry and bake in a moderate oven (350 degrees F.) two hours. Serves eight.

## FAMILY BREAST OF VEAL

1½ pounds breast of veal
1 onion, thinly sliced
2 tablespoons butter or drippings

6 small carrots
1½ cups tomato sauce, or canned tomato soup
Salt and pepper

Cut the veal into slices for serving, sprinkle each with salt and pepper, and dredge with flour. Pan-fry in butter or in drippings until they are well browned on both sides. Scrape the carrots and cut into quarters. In the bottom of the baking dish pour the tomato sauce; lay in the carrots, onions, and the veal. Cover and cook in a moderate oven (375 degrees F.) about three-quarters of an hour. Serve in the baking dish. Serves six.

## VEAL POTPIE

2 pounds veal neck or breast
2 small onions
6 small potatoes, diced
1 cup diced celery

1 cup diced carrots
3 tablespoons flour
Salt and pepper
Baking powder biscuits

Cut the veal into cubes and cover with hot salted water. Cook for thirty minutes. Add the vegetables and cook slowly until they are done. Season with salt and pepper. Thicken the liquid with flour smoothed in cold water. Pour into casserole and cover with baking powder biscuits and cook in a moderately hot oven (400 degrees F.) until the biscuits are done, about fifteen minutes. Serves six.

# VEGETABLE CASSEROLE DINNERS

California Starter Salad
Green Beans and Rice au Gratin
Whole Wheat Muffins and Butter
Baked Bananas with Top Milk or Cream
Coffee or Tea

❀

Mixed Fruit Juices
Lima Beans and Egg Casserole
Boston Brown Bread and Butter with Apple Butter
Tossed Green Salad
Coffee or Tea

❀

Corn and Cheese Soufflé
Potatoes boiled in Jackets
Garden Salad      Whole Wheat Crackers
Burnt Almond Ice Cream
Coffee or Tea

❀

Leek and Potato Soup with Triscuit
Eggplant with Cheese and Tomatoes
Raisin Bread and Butter
Stewed Fresh Fruits or Berries in Season
Cookies
Coffee or Tea

*Melon*
*Green Pepper Supper*
*Tossed Green Salad      Cheese Tray*
*Toasted Rolls and Butter*
*Apple Pie (with sour cream if liked)*
*Coffee or Tea*

*

*Lentils and Sausages*
*Western Fruit Plate*
*Hot Popovers and Butter*
*Brownies*
*Coffee or Tea*

*

*Stuffed Baked Onions*
*Asparagus with Cheese*
*French Bread and Butter*
*Old-fashioned Strawberry Shortcake*
*Coffee or Tea*

*

*Tomato Bouillon with Whole Wheat Crackers*
*Scalloped Peas and Eggs*
*Carrot and Potato Salad*
*Hot Rolls and Butter*
*Chocolate Macaroons*
*Coffee*

*Tomatoes stuffed with Mushrooms*
*Scalloped Potatoes*
*Endive Salad     Hot Rolls and Butter*
*Apricot Ice Cream and Brownies*
*Coffee or Tea*

## ASPARAGUS WITH CHEESE

Lay stalks of cooked asparagus in a shallow baking dish. Sprinkle with grated cheese, dot with butter, and bake in a moderate oven (375 degrees F.) until the cheese is melted and slightly browned.

## GREEN BEANS AND RICE AU GRATIN

1 ten-ounce box quick-frozen green beans
1 cup boiling salted water
½ cup finely diced onion
⅔ cup finely diced celery
2 tablespoons butter
1½ cups stewed tomatoes
¼ teaspoon celery salt
1¼ cups cooked rice
½ teaspoon sugar
Salt and pepper
4 tablespoons grated American cheese
3 tablespoons buttered bread crumbs

Drop frozen green beans into briskly boiling salted water, bring again to boiling, and boil eight to twelve minutes, or until just tender. Drain. Fry onion and celery in butter, covered, until tender but not browned. Add tomatoes, celery salt, rice, sugar, salt, and pepper. Turn into a greased casserole, and top with mixture of cheese and buttered crumbs. Place in a pan of hot water, and bake in hot oven (450 degrees F.) about twenty minutes, or until browned. Serves six to eight.

# BAKED BEANS

3 cups navy beans
¾ pound salt pork, sliced
1 tablespoon salt
1 small onion chopped
1 tablespoon dry mustard

½ cup brown sugar
2 tablespoons molasses
3 cups hot water, including
    water in which pork
    was boiled

Wash beans. Cover with water and soak overnight. Drain and cover with fresh water. Cook slowly until skins burst and the beans are very tender. Drain and place in a deep casserole or bean pot. Parboil the salt pork, place one piece deep inside the mixture and the other on top of the beans. Add three cups of liquid to which the seasonings have been added. Cover and bake in a slow oven (250 degrees F.) five hours. Uncover for another hour of baking. If necessary, add more liquid during the first part of the baking. Serves six to eight.

# BAKED LIMA BEANS

2 cups dried Lima beans,
    soaked overnight
2 sweet red peppers
Salt

2 cups cooked tomatoes
2 slices bacon

Drain the water from the beans, rinse in cold water; cover with fresh cold water, and heat slowly to boiling; then let simmer till tender. Drain. Turn a layer of the cooked beans into a casserole, cover with a layer of chopped sweet red pepper, season with salt. Add one slice of the bacon, chopped fine. Repeat the layer of beans and peppers and seasoning. Lay on the bacon, and then add the two cups of seasoned cooked tomatoes. Bake in a moderate oven (375 degrees F.) about two hours. Serves four to six.

## LIMA BEANS AND EGG CASSEROLE

1¼ cups dried Lima beans  
½ small onion  
Salt and pepper  
1½ tablespoons butter  
3 tablespoons flour  
1¼ cups milk  
1 cup grated American cheese  
2 to 3 hard-cooked eggs  
Buttered soft bread crumbs

Soak beans overnight in water. Add sliced onion, cover and cook over low heat until tender. Use just enough water so that there will be very little liquid remaining when beans are tender. Do not drain. Add one and one-fourth teaspoons of salt and a few grains of pepper near the end of the cooking time. Melt butter in a double boiler, add flour, and mix well. Add milk gradually and cook, stirring constantly until thickened. Add one-half cup of the cheese, stir until melted, and season with salt and pepper. Add Lima beans and sliced eggs, and pour into a buttered baking dish. Cover with crumbs mixed with remaining one-half cup of cheese. Bake in a moderate oven (350 degrees F.) about twenty-five minutes, or until cheese is melted and mixture is hot. Six servings.

## SCALLOPED LIMA BEANS

1 twelve-ounce box quick-frozen Lima beans  
2 cups boiling salted water  
6 strips bacon, cut in 1-inch pieces  
2 tablespoons minced onion  
1½ cups stewed tomatoes  
¾ teaspoon salt  
Dash of pepper  
1 cup buttered bread crumbs

Drop frozen Lima beans into briskly boiling salted water, bring again to boiling, and boil sixteen to eighteen minutes, or until just tender; drain. Cook bacon and onion until bacon is crisp; add tomatoes and seasonings, and bring to boiling. Place half of the beans in a small greased baking dish and cover with a layer of tomato mixture; repeat, using remaining beans and tomato mixture. Cover with crumbs. Bake uncovered in a moderate oven (350 degrees F.) twenty-five to thirty minutes, or until the crumbs are browned. Serves six.

## NAVY BEANS WITH TOMATOES

2 cups beans, soaked overnight    4 red-ripe tomatoes
2 tablespoons butter    Salt and pepper

Drain the soaked beans. Parboil for three minutes and drain again (saving the liquid for soup). Place the beans with tomatoes in a baking dish with two tablespoons of butter, and salt and pepper to season. Cook in a moderate oven (300 degrees F.) thirty minutes or a little longer. Top with crumbs for the last ten minutes, if you like. Serves four to six.

## CABBAGE OR CAULIFLOWER AU GRATIN

Cooked cauliflower or cabbage    Buttered bread crumbs
White Sauce    Grated cheese

Put either cooked cabbage or cauliflower in layers in a casserole, with a layer of White Sauce between. Cover the top with more sauce, buttered crumbs, and grated cheese. Set in a hot oven (350 degrees F.) until the sauce simmers and the top is brown.

## CAULIFLOWER AU GRATIN

1 small cauliflower (in flowerets)    ¾ teaspoon salt
     ⅛ teaspoon paprika
3 tablespoons quick-cooking tapioca    2 cups milk
     1 cup grated American cheese
1 cup bread crumbs, buttered

Cook cauliflower in boiling salted water twelve minutes, or until tender; drain and place in a large greased baking dish or in six small ones. Combine tapioca, salt, paprika, and milk in the top of a double boiler. Place over rapidly boiling water, and cook eight to ten minutes after the water boils again, stirring frequently. Remove from the boiling water; add cheese and stir until melted. Pour over hot cauliflower; cover with crumbs, and bake in moderate oven (350 degrees F.) twenty minutes. Serves six.

## CAULIFLOWER AND HAM SCALLOP

1 cauliflower
3 tablespoons butter or margarine
3 tablespoons flour
1½ cups milk

Salt and pepper
½ pound American cheese, shredded
1 cup chopped, cooked ham
1 cup buttered bread crumbs

Separate the cauliflower into flowerets and cook until slightly underdone. Make white sauce with the butter, flour, milk and seasonings. Add cheese and stir until melted. Place the cauliflower in a casserole, sprinkle it with the chopped ham and cover with the cheese sauce. Make a border of the buttered crumbs around the edge of the casserole. Bake in a moderate oven (350 degrees F.) twenty to thirty minutes, or until the crumbs are lightly browned. Serves six.

## CORN PUDDING

1 tablespoon butter, melted
1 tablespoon flour
1½ teaspoons salt
½ teaspoon sugar
⅛ teaspoon pepper
1½ cups rich milk

1 teaspoon scraped onion
1 tablespoon chopped pimiento
2 eggs, slightly beaten
1 ten-ounce box quick-frozen golden sweet corn, thawed

Combine butter, flour, salt, sugar, and pepper. Add milk slowly, stirring until smooth. Cook until thickened, stirring constantly. Remove from the fire, add onion, pimiento, eggs, and corn, and mix well. Turn into a baking dish. Set the dish in a pan of hot water, and bake in moderate oven (350 degrees F.) one hour, or until set. Serves four to six.

## CORN AND CHEESE SOUFFLÉ

2 tablespoons chopped onion
4 tablespoons butter
5 tablespoons flour
1¼ cups milk
¼ cup grated American cheese
1 ten-ounce box quick-frozen
    golden sweet corn,
    thawed

1 teaspoon salt
⅛ teaspoon pepper
¼ teaspoon Worcestershire
    Sauce
4 egg yolks, beaten until thick
    and lemon-colored
4 egg whites, stiffly beaten

Fry onion in butter until tender. Stir in the flour. Add milk and cook until thickened, stirring frequently. Add cheese and stir until the cheese is melted. Add corn, salt, pepper, and Worcestershire Sauce. Remove from the fire, add egg yolks, and mix well. Fold into egg whites. Turn into a greased casserole. Place in a pan of hot water and bake in a moderate oven (350 degrees F.) one hour, or until soufflé is firm. Serve with crisp broiled bacon, or sausages and broiled tomatoes. Serves six.

## EGGPLANT CASSEROLE

1 eggplant
1 green pepper
6 medium-sized onions

6 tomatoes sliced
1 teaspoon salt
½ teaspoon pepper

Pare and slice the eggplant and onions, and slice the green pepper. Fry in hot fat until brown. Then place the other vegetables in a greased casserole alternately with layers of sliced tomatoes. Season each layer with salt and pepper, and bake in a moderate oven (350 degrees F.) forty minutes. Serves six.

## EGGPLANT WITH CHEESE AND TOMATOES

| | |
|---|---|
| 1 eggplant | Salt and pepper |
| 1 onion, minced | Parmesan cheese, grated |
| 1 cup tomato pulp | Butter |
| ½ cup dry bread crumbs | |

Cut the eggplant in half. Bake in a moderate oven (375 degrees F.) until half done. Scoop out the pulp and chop fine. Fry the onions in butter, add the eggplant pulp and tomato pulp (no seeds). Cover and simmer till done. Bind with the crumbs, and season. Fill the eggplant shells with the mixture, sprinkle with cheese and a few bread crumbs, and dot with tiny pieces of butter on top. Place in a shallow flameproof baking dish and set under the broiler (not close to the flame) for about ten minutes until golden brown. Serves four to six.

## GREEN PEPPER SUPPER

| | |
|---|---|
| 8 large green peppers | 2 cups boiled rice |
| 1 onion | 16 shrimp, cooked and cleaned |
| 1 tablespoon curry powder | ½ cup bouillon, or chicken broth |
| 2 tablespoons butter | Rounds of buttered toast |

Plunge the peppers for a few minutes into boiling water, then cut off the tops and scoop out the seeds and fiber. Chop the onion fine, and cook in two tablespoons of butter with the curry powder. Do not brown but make sure the onion is softened. Add the rice, the shrimp cut into small pieces, and the bouillon or broth. Mix thoroughly, fill the peppers, adding salt if needed. Set the peppers on rounds of buttered toast in a buttered casserole, and let cook fifteen minutes in a hot oven (400 degrees F.) until very hot through. Serves eight.

Vary this recipe by mixing cooked sweetbreads into the rice and adding almonds in this case; or use leftover chicken or meat. Or omit the curry powder and mix one peeled red-ripe tomato into the cooking onions and butter.

## JERUSALEM ARTICHOKES AU GRATIN

2 cups sliced cooked Jerusalem    1 cup Béchamel or White Sauce
   artichokes    Bread crumbs
4 tablespoons grated cheese

Slice cooked Jerusalem artichokes and place them in a buttered baking dish with alternate layers of Béchamel or White Sauce. Sprinkle the top with bread crumbs and grated cheese. Dot with bits of butter, and bake in a hot oven (400 degrees F.) until the sauce simmers and is browned on top. Serves four to five.

## KALE AND CHEESE CASSEROLE

2 pounds kale    1¾ cups milk
2 teaspoons chopped onion    Salt and pepper
2½ tablespoons butter    Buttered soft bread crumbs
4½ tablespoons flour    1 cup grated American cheese

Remove any wilted leaves and tough stems from the kale, and wash thoroughly. Cook the kale and onion in a small quantity of boiling salted water in a covered pan until tender. Drain, and boil down the liquid to one-third cup. Melt the butter in a double boiler, add the flour, and mix well. Add the milk gradually and cook, stirring constantly until thickened. Add the kale liquid, and season with salt and pepper. Add the kale, and pour into a buttered baking dish. Cover with the crumbs mixed with the cheese, and bake in a moderate oven (350 degrees F.) about twenty-five minutes, or until the cheese is melted and the mixture is heated through. Six to eight servings.

## LENTILS AND SAUSAGES

| | |
|---|---|
| 2 cups lentils | 2 large onions |
| 6 small sausages, smoked variety | Salt and pepper |
| | Bouquet of parsley and bay leaf |

Wash lentils; look over carefully to remove small stones and dirt. Pour into a pan of boiling water and let them stand in this for half an hour. Drain and put in a saucepan of boiling salted water. Add the onions and the bouquet of herbs. Let simmer for two hours, then turn into a casserole; add the sausages pricked with a sharp fork, and continue cooking until the lentils are tender; drain off the liquor (keep for soup), and serve from the casserole. Enough for four to six.

## SAVORY POTATOES

| | |
|---|---|
| 2 pounds potatoes | 5 tablespoons grated cheese |
| 1 cup flour | Salt and paprika |
| 2 tablespoons butter | Bread crumbs |

Wash, peel, and boil about two pounds of potatoes; put them through a sieve or fine ricer. Sift one cup of flour into a dish, add the potatoes, and mix with the butter and two tablespoons of grated cheese; add salt and paprika.

Shape lightly into balls and lay on a sieve. Have ready some actively boiling salted water. Drop the potato shapes into it, a few at a time, and boil for fifteen minutes. When cooked, drain, place in a baking dish, dot with butter, sprinkle with grated cheese, and top with a light sprinkling of bread crumbs mixed with melted butter. Bake in a hot oven (425 degrees F.) ten minutes. Serves six.

## SCALLOPED MUSHROOMS

| | |
|---|---|
| 1½ pounds mushrooms | 1 egg yolk, beaten |
| ½ cup bouillon | 1 tablespoon sherry |
| ¼ cup butter | Salt |
| Lemon juice | |

Peel mushrooms and cut in large pieces. Throw them into boiling water for a few minutes, then into cold water to whiten them. Dry well, then pan-fry in hot butter. When almost tender, add the boiling hot bouillon and let simmer about ten minutes. Add lemon juice and seasoning to taste. Remove from the fire and add the beaten egg and sherry. Put into a casserole, dot with butter, and set in a hot oven (450 degrees F.) till thoroughly heated through. Serves six.

## STUFFED BAKED ONIONS

| | |
|---|---|
| 8 Spanish onions | ½ teaspoon pepper |
| 1 cup chopped nuts | 1 tablespoon chopped parsley |
| 1 cup dried bread crumbs | 1 egg, yolk only |
| ½ cup melted butter | 1 cup bouillon or water |
| ½ teaspoon salt | 1 tablespoon butter |
| 1 cup Cream Sauce or White Sauce | |

Peel the onions, and let cook in boiling water for one hour. When cooled a little, scoop out most of the center. Mix the chopped nuts, crumbs, butter, and seasonings into the beaten egg yolk, and then pile the mixture into the onion cases. Build up the top into dome shape. Set in a buttered casserole, pour in the bouillon, and bake in a moderate oven (375 degrees F.) forty-five minutes, basting occasionally with the liquid in the casserole, and last with the spoonful of butter in a little of the hot sauce in the casserole. When ready to serve, pour the Cream Sauce around the onions. Serves eight.

## SCALLOPED PEAS AND EGGS

1 twelve-ounce package quick-
    frozen peas
4 hard-cooked eggs
3 tablespoons butter or mar-
    garine
2 teaspoons minced onion

2½ tablespoons flour
1¼ cups milk
6 tablespoons vegetable liquor,
    or vegetable liquor and
    milk
Salt and pepper to taste

Cook quick-frozen peas according to directions on the box.
While cooking, melt butter in saucepan. Add onion and flour,
and stir to a paste. Add milk gradually, stirring constantly. Cook
two minutes or until thickened, stirring constantly. Measure
liquor drained from cooked vegetable, adding milk if necessary
to make up the amount. Add to sauce and blend. Season with salt
and pepper. Arrange seasoned drained peas, sauce, and sliced
eggs in alternate layers in a greased casserole. Sprinkle generously with buttered crumbs. Place in a pan of hot water, and
bake in hot oven (450 degrees F.) about twenty minutes, or
until browned. Serves four to six.

## POTATOES AND CHEESE

1 quart diced potatoes
1 grated onion
3 slivered pimientos
1 pint scalded milk

2 tablespoons cornstarch
1 teaspoon salt
½ teaspoon pepper
½ pound American cheese

Cook potatoes, onion, and pimientos five minutes in boiling
salted water. Then drain. Make a sauce of the milk, cornstarch,
and seasonings, and into it crumble the cheese. Cook till the
cheese is melted. Put the potato mixture in a baking dish, cover
with the sauce, and bake in a moderate oven (350 degrees F.)
forty-five minutes. Serves six.

## SPINACH AU GRATIN

1 peck (2½ to 3 pounds) spin-   Salt and pepper
   ach, washed carefully   ¾ cup grated cheese
1 cup White Sauce   ⅔ cup cracker crumbs
   ⅛ cup melted butter

After the spinach is clean, cook till tender, and then chop fine. Butter a baking dish, and spread a layer of the cooked spinach in it. Season with salt and pepper. Over this pour White Sauce, a little of the grated cheese, and continue the layers until the dish is full. Make the top layer of the cheese and the crumbs mixed with the melted butter. Set the dish in a moderate oven (375 degrees F.) till the top is well browned. Serves six.

## PARSNIPS WITH CHEESE

Prepare cooked parsnips after the above recipe, omitting the cracker crumbs and butter, and topping the casserole simply with grated cheese.

## CANDIED SWEET POTATOES

4 sweet potatoes, parboiled   Powdered sugar
1 cup molasses and maple   3 tablespoons butter
   syrup, mixed   1 slice pineapple, cut in cubes
   Salt

Peel and slice the potatoes. Pan-fry in the butter, and place in a shallow baking dish. Sprinkle with salt. Dot with two table-spoons of butter, and pour the molasses and maple syrup over this. Dot with remaining butter, and bake uncovered in a moderate oven (375 degrees F.) twenty minutes. Ten minutes before removing from the oven, place the small pieces of pineapple on top of the potatoes, sprinkle with sugar, and continue baking. Serves four.

## SCALLOPED SWEET POTATOES AND APPLES

6 boiled sweet potatoes          1½ cups sliced apples
½ cup brown sugar                ¼ cup butter
                    ½ teaspoon salt

Drain, peel, and slice potatoes in one-fourth-inch pieces. Put a layer of sweet potatoes in a buttered baking dish, then a layer of apples. Sprinkle with sugar and salt, and dot with butter. Repeat until the dish is filled, with the top layer of apples. Sprinkle this with sugar. Bake in a moderate oven (350 degrees F.) fifty minutes. Serves six.

## SWEET POTATOES AND APPLES

Boil sweet potatoes in their jackets. Peel and slice in fairly thick slices. Pare, core, and slice an equal quantity of cooking apples. Butter a deep casserole, and put in alternate layers of potatoes and apples, sprinkling each layer with a little sugar and salt. Dot each thickly with butter. Cover the dish, and set in a moderate oven (350 degrees F.) ten minutes, then remove cover and bake slowly (300 degrees F.) until the apples are cooked.

Vary by using diced canned pineapple in this recipe and pouring pineapple juice over all before the baking begins. Serves six.

## SWEET POTATO PUDDING

6 sweet potatoes               ¼ cup cream, heated
3 tablespoons butter           ⅛ cup whisky, or ¼ cup sherry
                    Salt and pepper

Boil potatoes until tender. Drain them, and mash with one tablespoon of butter. Beat well and slowly add the cream. Beat until fluffy. Add two tablespoons of butter, the whisky or sherry, and put the mixture into a buttered baking dish. Set in a moderate oven (350 degrees F.) twenty minutes until brown. Serves six.

## TOMATOES STUFFED WITH MUSHROOMS

6 red-ripe tomatoes
1 tablespoon parsley, chopped fine
1 tablespoon celery, chopped fine
3 tablespoons butter
¼ teaspoon marjoram, chopped
¼ cup mushrooms, browned in butter and minced
2 tablespoons green peppers, chopped
Salt and pepper to taste
Bread crumbs

Peel tomatoes, cut off stem ends, and scoop out the centers. Season the inside of each. Melt half the butter; when it begins to brown add the green pepper and simmer several minutes. Press tomato pulp and juice through a sieve, and add to the mushrooms which have been browned in butter and finely chopped. Add seasoning to taste, and mix all together thoroughly. Fill tomatoes with the mixture, and place in a well-buttered baking dish; sprinkle with bread crumbs and dot with the remaining butter. Bake in a moderate oven (375 degrees F.) about thirty minutes. Serves six.

## WHO SAID CHAFING DISHES ARE QUAINT?

The chafing dish disappeared from the American home about the time that streamlined kitchen ranges—and efficiency in home-making—came into being. Before that, the little alcohol-heated saucepan of silver or nickel on its twirly legs had served as a beau-catcher for sister, providing an easy way for her to show off her cookery skill on Sunday night or any evening after a concert. In the proper setting and with a carefully executed chicken à la king (mixed in the kitchen that morning by old Addie) or a Welsh rarebit, the swain of the Nineties practically fell at her feet after the first mouthful. He, poor dear, blindly assumed that she could also bake a cherry pie—and all else which was implied in that charming symbolism.

What might have happened to this country without this culinary aid to romance is not pleasant to contemplate. How many old maid aunts today can blame their condition on the fact that father simply would not have a spirit lamp in the house! How many fond mothers (the girls who *did* have chafing dishes) can chuckle over how easy it was in those days to catch a man! Whatever *is* the matter with the girls today?

One thing is certain they need not go without a chafing dish, for there is a well-marked revival of interest in table cookery. Partly because many small city apartments have only the most meager of kitchenette space and it is easier to cook some of the meal at the table. Partly because, with the revival of Victorian styles in house decoration and clothing, there are unmistakable signs of a return to the Nineties in graciousness of table settings and accessories. Also there is a heightened interest in gourmet cookery, stimulated just before the war by the appearance of a number of books as well as articles in smart magazines on the "little dinners" of Mrs. So-and-So, whose cook was a Russian, or Hungarian, or the only remaining member of the oldest family in some walled city of the Pyrenees.

And at the same time the American and European wine dealers launched a campaign to interest Americans in a more subtle appreciation of their products depicting, in well-placed magazine advertisements the joys of dining at home in a charming setting, the lady of the house playing hostess to the extent of doing a little cooking right under the noses of her guests.

Far from being a toy of only slightly accomplished cooks, actually the "spirit stove" was one of the most valuable assets of the great chefs of the Eighties and Nineties in Paris and London. Alexis Soyer, the charming Frenchman who was one of the most famous of that profession, perfected a new table stove which won him acclaim and considerable money. He knew, as did his colleagues in the great kitchens of Europe, that certain sauces ought to be made just before they are added to the fish or chicken, to a soufflé or a well-turned roast.

The history of the achievements of the handy little device for cooking at the table is long and interesting. And its modern version (with an electric plate) as well as with the compact and improved alcohol and canned heat arrangements, can help make simple home cooking very pleasant.

The evening planned around a chafing dish supper is bound to run more smoothly if you own a large tray on which you can arrange every item needed in the cooking, every spoon and fork, salt shaker, and condiment bottle. The tray should be big enough to hold the bowl of chicken or cheese, the eggs, milk, cream, or a little wine, or whatever else is called for in the recipe.

In the midst of all, also on the tray, and exactly where you can reach it with the most ease, is the chafing dish.

The kind you select is a matter of personal taste and pocketbook—and what you can find in the shops. You will need one with a water compartment beneath the cooking pan; if possible, own two chafing dishes: one with a porcelain-lined cooking pan and another of metal.

Many chafing dish luncheons or suppers consist only of the hot entrée and coffee and dessert; you may add a salad or not, as you please.

The Victorian revival has brought back those little aprons too, and delicate tablecloths, exquisite old silver and frail china. Maybe the girls of the Nineties were right. Most men like a spot of quiet in the busy week, with a plate of delicious eggs or chicken, cheese or sausages, fragrant coffee afterwards and a luscious cake. ("I baked it myself!") After all, it is always open season for beau-catching.

## CHAFING DISH MENUS

Welsh Rarebit with Buttered Toast
Tossed Green Salad
Apple Tarts with Ice Cream
Coffee

❋

Frizzled Beef à la King
Wild Rice     Buttered Hot Rolls
Garden Salad     Cheese
Black Walnut Ice Cream
Coffee

❋

Tongue Supper
Buttered String Beans
Potato Salad
Orange Spongecake     Chocolate Ice Cream
Coffee

❋

Hungarian Supper
Garden Salad     Cottage Cheese
Pumpernickel and Butter
Angel Pie
Coffee

Peas Breton     Cold Cuts
Cheese
Carrot and Potato Salad
Orange Refrigerator Cake
Coffee

✿

Broiled Tomatoes and Peppers
Baked Beans with Crisp Bacon Top
Boston Brown Bread and Butter
Baked Apples
Coffee

✿

Appetizer Tray of Raw Carrot Straws, Olives, Celery
Chicken à la King
Hot Biscuits or Toast
Blackberry Tart with Ice Cream
Coffee

✿

Breasts of Chicken
Buttered Peas
Artichoke Hearts and Tomato Salad
Raisin Cake
Coffee

✿

Hotsy Totsy Chicken on Toast
Tossed Green Salad
Orange Refrigerator Cake
Coffee

*Chicken Livers in Wine*
*Buttered Toasted Whole Wheat Rolls*
*Romaine and Grapefruit Salad*
*Swedish Apple Pudding*
*Coffee*

❋

*Night Life Eggs on Buttered Toast*
*Tossed Green Salad*
*Apple Tarts*
*Coffee*

❋

*Finnan Haddie on Fried Mush*
*Spring Salad Platter*
*Bread and Butter*
*Coffee*

❋

*Lobster Newburgh on Toast*
*Salad Bowl*
*Sherbet and Cookies*
*Coffee*

❋

*Oysters Claremont*
*Buttered Toasted Rolls*
*Cranberry Mousse*
*Coffee*

*Oyster Stew*
*Buttered Toasted Rolls*
*Raisin Cake*
*Coffee*

❋

*Oyster Supper*
*Buttered Toast*
*Cheese and Crackers*
*Coffee*

❋

*Clubman's Shrimp with Rice*
*Refrigerator Cheesecake*
*Coffee*

❋

*Creamed Eggs*
*Toasted Rolls and Butter*
*Baked Peaches     Devil's Food Cake*
*Coffee*

❋

*Plain French Omelet*
*Scalloped Potatoes*
*Sliced Tomatoes with Thick French Dressing*
*Bread and Butter*
*Strawberry-Raspberry Dessert*
*Coffee*

*Creamed Scrambled Eggs with Chives*
*Buttered Toast*
*Fruit Tarts with Cream*
*Coffee*

## CURRY OF ANYTHING

Make a simple curry sauce by adding one tablespoon of curry powder to the White Sauce made with one tablespoon flour, one tablespoon butter, one-half teaspoon salt, and one cup milk. Heat cleaned cooked shrimp in this, or lobster, chicken, or oysters (cook the latter till they are plump and the edges curling).

The garnish is important in serving curry; grated fresh coconut, ground peanuts, Major Gray's Chutney, Indian relish, Bombay duck (or dried salt fish), mustard pickles, rings of crisp French-fried onions, grated hard-cooked eggs (yolks and whites separate). If Bombay duck is not procurable, spread crisp crackers with anchovy paste and toast them in the oven. These are broken in crumbs on top of the serving of curry.

It adds much to the service of a curry if Oriental wares can be used: Chinese dishes and accessories give the proper atmosphere. But a good curry tastes fine off any plate.

## FRIZZLED BEEF À LA KING

½ pound dried beef                Salt and pepper
1 cup mushroom caps, sliced       ½ cup butter
1 green pepper, chopped           2 tablespoons flour
1 pimiento, chopped               2 cups rich milk
¼ cup sherry

Before the party, place one-half of the butter in a saucepan and heat the mushrooms, green peppers, and pimiento in this until soft. Put the dried beef in a little cold water and let stand

one-half hour. Squeeze the beef dry. Pull apart into small pieces.
Melt one-half the butter in the chafing dish and add beef, stirring occasionally until the beef is cooked. Add flour, sprinkling
it over the meat. Stir until absorbed by the butter. Add milk
slowly and bring to boiling, stirring constantly. Reduce heat and
simmer ten minutes. Add the cooked mushroom mixture and stir
until well blended. Remove from the fire and add sherry, stirring
it well through the mixture. Add salt and pepper, depending on
the saltiness of the beef. Serve with wild rice. Serves four.

## ITALIAN LAMB CHOPS

Trim chops, dip into beaten egg in which one tablespoon of
water has been mixed, then into bread crumbs mixed with half
as much grated cheese.

Pan-fry in the hot chafing dish (a metal one) in which a little
butter has been melted. Brown well on all sides. Season with salt
and pepper. Serve with a very thin slice of lemon on each chop.

## TONGUE SUPPER

| | |
|---|---|
| 1 egg yolk, beaten slightly | 2 tablespoons olive oil |
| 2 teaspoons French mustard | ½ lemon, juice only |
| ½ teaspoon curry powder | 8 slices cold boiled tongue |
| 6 drops Tabasco Sauce | ¾ cup bread crumbs |

To the beaten egg add the mustard, condiments, and the oil
and lemon juice. Dip the slices of tongue in this, then roll in the
bread crumbs until thickly coated. Melt a little butter in the
chafing dish and pan-fry the tongue slices until they are browned
on both sides. Serve with a hot green vegetable. Serves four, or
eight if the slices are large.

## HUNGARIAN SUPPER (Pre-war)
### (Start this one before the guests arrive.)

2 pounds lean veal
½ cup butter
4 large onions
1 clove garlic
1 can tomatoes
1 heaping teaspoon salt
½ teaspoon freshly ground black
    pepper

1 teaspoon paprika
1 teaspoon grated nutmeg
½ teaspoon mace
1 tablespoon sugar
1 cup sour cream
2 tablespoons flour

Melt the butter in a large chafing dish, add sliced onions and chopped garlic; cook until soft but do not brown. Add the veal cut in two-inch cubes and sear on all sides. Add seasoning and tomatoes. Simmer until veal is tender.

About fifteen minutes before serving, add sour cream and thicken with two tablespoons of flour stirred smoothly into the sauce. Serve with hot rice, noodles, or macaroni. Serves eight.

## PEAS BRETON

1 tablespoon butter
4 cups young green peas
1 sprig mint
2 slices onion

1 teaspoon sugar
Nutmeg
Salt
White pepper

Lettuce

Melt butter in the chafing dish; add peas and seasonings; stir together; add mint and onion, and cover all with freshly washed lettuce leaves. Cover tightly with the lid and let steam and simmer over a low fire until the peas are tender. They may be cooked the same way in a casserole in the oven. Serves six or more.

## BROILED TOMATOES WITH PEPPERS

Melt butter in the chafing dish; in the hot butter, lay slices of red-ripe tomatoes cut an inch thick and sprinkled with finely cut green peppers as well as with salt and pepper. Pan-fry until cooked on one side; turn, cover the slices with butter and peppers from the pan and continue cooking, spooning the sauce in the pan over the cooking tomato.

## TURKISH PILAF

1 cup rice
1½ cups hot bouillon or stock
1 cup canned tomato soup

1 teaspoon salt
½ teaspoon paprika
½ cup butter

Blanch the rice, add the stock and tomato soup, salt, and paprika, and let cook until the rice is tender. Add the butter and mix through the rice with a silver fork. Serves four.

## CHICKEN À LA KING

2 cups cooked chicken
6 to 8 mushrooms
1 sweet green pepper
2 tablespoons butter

Paprika
2 cups cream
3 egg yolks
Wineglass of sherry

Salt and white pepper

Cut cold boiled fowl in small pieces, removing all skin, fat, and gristle. Slice the mushrooms after they have been cleaned and peeled (use silver knife). Wash the green pepper and remove seeds; mince. Put the butter in the chafing dish, add mushrooms, and cook five minutes; then add the peppers and cook a few more minutes. Put in the chicken, seasoning, and cream.

When boiling, lift from the hot fire, and stir in rapidly the yolks of the eggs beaten smooth with two tablespoons of cream.

Do not allow the mixture to boil after adding the eggs, but heat until the eggs thicken. Add the sherry, and stir. Serve at once on toast. Serves five or six.

## BREASTS OF CHICKEN

2 chicken breasts, removed
    from bone
2 small slices Virginia ham
10 small fresh mushrooms
        3 or 4 tablespoons butter

1 teaspoon salt
¼ teaspoon white pepper
¼ teaspoon paprika
1½ cups sweet cream

Heat butter in chafing dish; fry chicken breasts until slightly brown; add the ham cut into four pieces, the mushrooms, salt, and other seasonings. Pour in the cream. Cover and cook gently until the liquid is reduced one-third and the meat is tender. Serve on hot rice or simply in its gravy. Serves four.

## HOTSY TOTSY CHICKEN

That is a silly name, but the hostess who serves it to me—I am glad to say on many occasions—calls it that, and who am I to change an inspired cook's title?

2 cups cooked chicken, cubed
1 cup cooked peas
½ teaspoon salt
¼ teaspoon freshly ground black
    pepper
1 teaspoon onion juice
        1 cup cream

1 pimiento, cut in small pieces
1 teaspoon lemon juice
¼ cup butter
¼ cup flour
½ teaspoon salt
1 cup chicken broth

Mix the chicken, peas, salt, pepper, onion juice, lemon juice, and pimiento, and set aside in a cool place to marinate. Make a cream sauce in the chafing dish by melting the butter, stirring the flour smoothly into it, then the seasonings, cream, and broth.

Stir until smooth. Add the marinated ingredients and let stand over the hot water to become very hot. Serve on buttered toast points. Serves six.

## CHICKEN WITH ALMONDS

| | |
|---|---|
| 2 small chickens, or 1 large one | 4 cups water |
| 1 tablespoon vinegar | 1 tablespoon salt |

Wash and clean the dressed and cleaned chicken inside and out. Rub with the vinegar (or lemon juice) inside and out. Let boil slowly till tender. Skim off the fat. Let cool, and cut meat from the bones.

### Sauce

| | |
|---|---|
| 1 tablespoon butter | ¾ cup almonds, shredded or |
| 2 tablespoons flour | chopped |
| 4 cups stock (or bouillon) | ½ cup cream |
| 2 tablespoons horseradish | |

Blanch and chop the almonds very fine. Mix butter and flour in the chafing dish and, when blended, add the cream and stock, and stir well; add almonds, and heat thoroughly. Season, and add the horseradish. Add the chicken; heat through. Serve with rice or delicately seasoned noodles. Serves six.

## CHICKEN SHORTCAKE

Using the chafing dish, heat leftover chicken in gravy or a rich white sauce seasoned with salt, pepper, and a little mace. Add a few mushrooms which have been cooked in butter.

Meanwhile have ready a hot shortcake biscuit made by mixing your best biscuit dough, patting it into two layers, and spreading one thickly with butter. Put the layers together and bake until golden brown. Separate, and spread the lower one with the hot creamed chicken. Put on the top layer, and cover with more of the heated chicken and gravy.

If baking biscuit dough is out of the question (as it often is in the kitchenless household), use rolls from the bakery or English muffins or toast.

## CHICKEN LIVERS IN WINE

24 chicken livers      Salt and pepper
Butter      1½ cups Madeira Sauce

Soak livers for fifteen minutes in water. Rinse, cut into thirds, salt and pepper them, and cook in the chafing dish in a little butter. Strain, and add Madeira Sauce; heat through but do not let the sauce boil. Serve with freshly boiled rice.

### Madeira Sauce

2 tablespoons butter    1 onion, sliced
2 tablespoons flour    1 carrot, sliced
3 cups meat stock or consommé    ½ cup Madeira
2 tablespoons tomato purée (or    Bouquet of parsley, thyme, and
    canned tomato soup)      bay leaf
1 fresh tomato peeled and    Salt and pepper
    quartered

Melt butter, stir in the flour, and gradually add the stock, heating and stirring until smooth; bring to boiling and add tomato purée, quartered fresh tomato, sliced onion, carrot, the bouquet of herbs, salt, and pepper. Stir well and let simmer very gently two hours, stirring occasionally. By this time the sauce should be reduced at least one-fourth and be fairly thick. Strain, bring to boiling again and reduce more, and more quickly. Add the Madeira, and cook two to three minutes without boiling.

Prepare sauce before time to cook the chicken livers at the table.

The recipes for livers and sauce serve six.

## NIGHT LIFE EGGS

1 large onion
1 cup milk
3 hard-cooked eggs, coarsely chopped
Lemon juice
Rounds of buttered toast
4 slices red-ripe tomato, seasoned and fried in butter

2 egg yolks
1 teaspoon minced parsley
2 tablespoons grated cheese
⅛ teaspoon paprika
½ teaspoon salt
Cayenne

Slice and fry the onion in butter in the chafing dish. When brown, add the milk and the hard-cooked eggs, and stir over low heat for five minutes.

Meanwhile have ready: the beaten yolks of the two eggs, minced parsley, grated cheese, and seasonings; add to the onion mixture and stir over a low heat for seven to eight minutes longer. Add the lemon juice, about a dessertspoonful, just before serving. Serve very hot on rounds of buttered toast on which there is a fried slice of seasoned tomato. Serves four.

## EGGS ON ANCHOVY TOAST

Clove of garlic
2 heaping tablespoons of butter
1 cup cream

5 well-beaten eggs
½ teaspoon celery salt
¼ teaspoon paprika

Rounds of toast spread with anchovy paste and butter

Rub the chafing dish (over hot water) with the cut clove of garlic. Then put in the two heaping tablespoons of butter and the cream. When this is hot, pour in the well-beaten eggs seasoned with the celery salt and paprika. Stir rapidly until the eggs are a thick custard. Heap at once on the rounds of prepared toast. Serves four.

## FINNAN HADDIE ON FRIED MUSH

Flake finnan haddie and let it simmer, not boil, in a little cream or rich milk.

Make a White Sauce in the chafing dish, following the standard recipe and adding paprika as a finish. When it is cooked and medium thick, add the finnan haddie, and when heated through serve on rounds or squares of hot fried mush.

## NEWBURGH

It doesn't have to be lobster to be a Newburgh. Use cleaned cooked shrimp, chicken, crab flakes, finnan haddie, any cooked fish, sweetbreads.

| | |
|---|---|
| 1 teaspoon butter | 1 cup thin cream |
| 1 tablespoon flour | 2 cups fish or chicken, etc. |
| ¼ teaspoon salt | 2 egg yolks |
| ¼ teaspoon paprika | ¼ cup sherry |

In the chafing dish, make a sauce of the first five ingredients; when smooth, add the fish or chicken cut in small pieces as uniform as possible; mix and let stand over boiling water until very hot. Stir in the beaten yolks, then stir in the wine and serve at once on toast. Serves four to six.

## LOBSTER NEWBURGH

| | |
|---|---|
| 2 medium-sized boiled lobsters, or 2 cups lobster meat | 1 wineglass sherry or Madeira |
| 4 tablespoons butter | 1 cup cream |
| 1 level tablespoon flour | 3 eggs |
| 2 saltspoons paprika | 2 tablespoons cream |
| | Toast cut in triangles |

Put butter in the chafing dish directly over the heat; as it melts, add the lobster meat and toss lightly with a silver fork; when the butter begins to assume a pinkish color (in about two minutes) add one level tablespoon of flour, smoothing it into the butter; then add the paprika and the wine. Cook five minutes; then add one cup of cream and let come to boiling. Beat the yolks of three eggs with the two tablespoons of cream. Stir in quickly and remove from the heat as soon as thickened. Do not allow to boil actively. Serve on thin toast points. Serves four to five or even six.

## OYSTERS CLAREMONT

½ cup butter
1 teaspoon English mustard
Salt, pepper, celery salt
    (about ¼ teaspoon each)
1½ cups celery, chopped fine

3 cups rich cream
2 dozen oysters
2 tablespoons sherry or
    Madeira

In a chafing dish pan, put the butter and the English mustard; add salt, pepper, and celery salt. Stir until the butter melts. Add the finely chopped celery and stir frequently until it is nearly cooked. Then pour the cream in slowly while stirring. Allow to come to the boiling point, stirring all the time. Add the cleaned oysters, and cook about five minutes, then add the sherry or wine. Serve on very hot plates, garnished with parsley. Serves six.

## PANNED OYSTERS

36 oysters
2 tablespoons butter

Salt and pepper
Flour

Put oysters in a colander and wash by letting the cold water run over and through them. Drain for ten minutes. Discard liquor and water. Heat the chafing dish pan (not a porcelain-

lined one), and when it is very hot put butter and oysters in it
Shake and stir until the oysters bubble and the edges curl. Sea-
son. Dredge oysters lightly with flour. Serve in a hot dish at once.
Serves six to eight.

## OYSTER STEW

3 pints milk
2 tablespoons flour
1 tablespoon crackers crushed
    to fine crumbs

Salt and pepper
1 quart oysters
2 tablespoons butter

Heat milk in the chafing dish. Add a little cold water to the
flour and cracker crumbs, and mix smoothly; then stir into the
hot milk, and cook six minutes. Add seasonings and oysters, and
cook until the oysters are puffed. Add butter and serve at once.
Serves six.

## OYSTER SUPPER

2 tablespoons butter
Clove of garlic
1 tablespoon flour
1 tablespoon Worcestershire
    Sauce

Juice of 1 lemon
Salt and paprika
1 pint of oysters with liquor
3 tablespoons sherry

Rub the chafing dish with the pricked garlic clove; add butter
and let melt, then stir in the flour smoothly; add Worcestershire,
lemon juice, salt, and paprika. Into this, stir the strained and
heated oyster liquor. When smooth, add oysters and cook until
they are plump and the edges begin to curl. Then add the sherry
and serve at once on toast. Serves four.

*A variation of this is:*

Omit sherry and lemon from the above recipe and add one
tablespoon Harvey Sauce when the hot oyster liquor is added;

then add two well-beaten egg yolks to one cup cream; cook the oysters in this sauce until they are plump and their edges curl. Serves four to six.

## CLUBMAN'S SHRIMP

2 pounds freshly cooked shrimp
2 fresh tomatoes, peeled and cut in cubes
3 large shallots, chopped fine
1 small clove of garlic, chopped fine
Salt, pepper, cayenne

¼ cup white wine
2 cups rich tomato sauce (canned soup may be used)
1 tablespoon olive oil
2 ounces butter
Parsley, chopped fine

Heat the olive oil in a chafing dish, add shallots and garlic, then add the cleaned shrimp seasoned with salt, pepper, and cayenne. Let cook a few minutes, then add the tomatoes; cover, and simmer five minutes; add the tomato sauce, and cook fifteen minutes. Add the wine and stir through; then remove from the heat and stir in the butter and parsley. Serve at once with freshly cooked rice, or without it. Serves six.

## WELSH RAREBIT

1 tablespoon butter
½ pound cheese (American Cheddar, old) cut in small pieces

¼ saltspoon salt
¼ teaspoon mustard
Cayenne
⅛ to ½ cup ale or beer

1 egg

Put the butter in a chafing dish (over hot water); when melted, add cheese and seasonings. As cheese melts, add ale gradually, stirring constantly; then add the egg slightly beaten. Serve on thin crackers or bread toasted on one side only. Serves four.

## CREAMED EGGS

6 hard-cooked eggs
2 cups Medium White Sauce
1 tablespoon minced parsley
    Sprigs of parsley
1 teaspoon Worcestershire
    Sauce
6 rounds buttered toast

Cut the eggs in quarters. Place in the chafing dish and add the White Sauce, parsley, and Worcestershire. Heat over hot water. Arrange the toast on plates, cover with the egg mixture. Garnish with parsley.

Various good things may be added to this recipe. Try chopped chives in place of the parsley; one-half to one cup minced left-over cooked ham; one cup grated cheese added to the White Sauce before pouring it over the eggs; one-half to one cup minced cooked tongue or dried beef; a few tablespoons crisp chopped bacon; two chopped boned anchovies; three or four tablespoons chopped olives. Serves four to six.

## CRÊPES SUZETTE

To make these thin pancakes, so delicious for dessert, use:

2 cups flour
¾ cup powdered sugar
5 eggs
2 cups milk
Salt
Grated lemon or orange peel

Mix together the flour, salt, and sugar. Add the milk slowly, forming a thick paste. Add the well-beaten eggs and mix thoroughly. Add the grated peel. Fry on a hot buttered chafing dish pan or griddle, making the cakes small and thin, and frying until almost crisp—but just soft enough to roll.

Have ready the following sauce:

2 tangerines
6 tablespoons butter
1 cup powdered sugar
Curaçao

Beat the butter and add the sugar gradually, creaming together. Add the grated rind of the tangerines and the juice, a little at a time, stirring all the while so as not to curdle the mixture. Add a few drops of curaçao if you like.

Spread a spoonful of this sauce over each pancake and roll it deftly with the spoon.

The crêpes may be cooked in the kitchen, brought to the table with the sauce, and then heated in the chafing dish. Spread them with the sauce and serve them at the table. Enough for four to six.

## SCRAMBLED EGGS

| | |
|---|---|
| 6 eggs slightly beaten | ⅛ teaspoon pepper |
| ½ cup thin cream | 2 tablespoons butter |
| ¼ teaspoon salt | 2 tablespoons chopped chives (optional) |

Make this in the upper part of the chafing dish, over hot water. Combine the slightly beaten eggs, cream, and seasonings. Melt the butter in the pan. Pour in the egg mixture and cook slowly. As the eggs become firm, scrape from the bottom of the pan. Continue this until the mixture is thick and creamy. Serve at once on thin toast or with crisp bacon or sausage. Serves four to six.

## SALADS

The informality of casserole and chafing dish meals is ideal for serving salads which not only contribute notably to the color and hunger-satisfying essentials of such occasions, but the tossed green salad, raw vegetable combination, or plate of fruits (fruit salad as served on the West Coast) are health builders. With such salads in our daily meals our own health is improved; also, we are helping to raise the country's nutrition ratio—something we've heard a great deal about since the beginning of the war.

But eating a salad should not be done as a duty, stoking the greens in until the cheeks bulge and the whole idea of grass and fodder eating brings on a bunny-in-the-cage complex. (Haven't you noticed that some people who subsist largely on raw greens look more than slightly like rabbits?) The salad can be as pleasurable a part of the meal as the succulent meat or the tender rich cake served at the end.

Serve the salad attractively. The popular salad bowls today harmonize with every type of casserole you are likely to have in your establishment. It is up to you whether you prefer a wooden bowl and have a place to keep it and will season and take care of it; or whether you mix salad in an earthenware or glass bowl; or whether it is mixed in the kitchen and served on plates before it is brought to the table.

As with the casseroles, shop around until you find a bowl which pleases your taste, and which is at home with the casseroles you are going to use on the table and with the plates and other wares you like for luncheons and suppers. Select a mixing fork and spoon to harmonize with the bowl. If you decide on a wooden set, it is only necessary to drain the bowl after each use and wipe with a clean damp cloth; do not wash it. Keep it covered with waxed paper or one of the pliofilm covers designed for refrigerator use, or turn the bowl upside down. Wipe with a clean damp cloth again before mixing a new salad in it.

For any salad, use only the freshest greens and vegetables available. Wash all leafy salads with extreme care to remove both creatures and sand. One gritty mouthful is enough not only to ruin the occasion for most guests (and enrage the family too) but also to make your reputation as a hostess something less flattering than you would like it.

Wash the salad greens under running water over and over again until the leaves are absolutely clean. Discard dark edges, spotted leaves, and otherwise damaged ones. Let them stand in a colander to drain. Then crisp them in the refrigerator, in the drawer especially designed for this, or lacking such a compartment, wrap the greens loosely in a clean tea towel and place in a cold part of the refrigerator.

At serving time, do the mixing. Avoid fancy-cut knives for the carrots, cucumbers, radishes, and any other solid vegetables. Either scrape them slightly if they are coarse-skinned or score with the tines of a fork, then slice crosswise or in thin, long strips.

Don't use garlic or onion unless you are sure their flavors are welcome to all who will share the salad. It is easy enough to ask about this before you mix it.

Experiment with dressings.

Experiment with herbs. Both dried and fresh herbs are increasingly available today. Grow your own if you have a garden or a kitchen window box. There are books written on herb growing and herb cookery, and on the health and gustatory reasons for adding these little plants to our daily diet. Don't use them recklessly; they have subtle, interesting, and provocative personalities, some of them very bold, and they demand understanding in order to give their best to any mixture.

There are deliciously flavored vinegars tasting of herbs, mint, horseradish, and other ingredients, and wine vinegars to vary salad dressings. They give them new tang and substance. Onion salt, garlic salt, celery salt, poppy seed (for potato salad), peppercorns to be freshly ground in your small pepper mill: these are available in the larger cities at not only the grocers but in the special food shops of the housefurnishing stores and of the big department stores and, in some cases, even in the book and gift shops. If you can't find them in your community, peruse the small advertisements in the handsome home decorating and gardening magazines and in the fashion journals, because the small de luxe shops on Madison Avenue and the cross-town streets of New York, and the famous housewares stores are usually to be found among the advertisers. Such shops will send their wares by mail anywhere, no matter if you live in Shangri-La.

With or without these herbs and seasoned vinegars and the accessories which are daily becoming more popular in good cookery, the important things to remember are to have any salad cold, the dressing delicious, and not to forget to chill the salad plates.

## ASPARAGUS VINAIGRETTE

Cook asparagus until tender. Chill or serve warm with this dressing:

½ cup olive oil
¼ cup tarragon vinegar
1 teaspoon chervil, chopped
½ teaspoon chives, chopped
¼ teaspoon parsley, chopped

¼ teaspoon salt
Pepper, to taste
1 teaspoon tarragon, chopped
1 small sour pickle, chopped
    very fine
1 teaspoon capers, chopped

Combine all and mix thoroughly. Add a little finely chopped hard-cooked egg to the top of each serving. Enough for four salads.

## ARTICHOKE HEARTS AND TOMATO SALAD

2 to 4 artichoke hearts for each serving

Watercress

2 or 3 quarters red-ripe tomatoes for each serving

French Dressing

Use canned artichoke hearts, rinsed and chilled in the refrigerator. Peel tomatoes and cut into quarters. Dress with French Dressing, and let stand a few minutes while you arrange crisp, clean watercress on a salad plate. Arrange artichokes and tomatoes, add a little more French Dressing. One serving.

## CARROT AND POTATO SALAD

2 cups diced cooked potatoes

3 cups grated raw carrot

1 tablespoon minced onion

¼ cup chopped watercress

1 cup mayonnaise

Salt and pepper

Lettuce

Watercress sprigs

Combine potatoes, carrots, onion, chopped watercress, and real mayonnaise; season with salt and pepper. Arrange on lettuce; garnish with watercress. Serves four to six.

## CHEF'S CALIFORNIA SALAD BOWL

½ lettuce head

1 bunch romaine

1 bunch watercress

½ head chicory

12 or more raw spinach leaves

2 cups sliced California oranges

½ cup ham slivers

½ cup celery slivers

2 hard-cooked eggs

½ cup Lemon French Dressing

Cut or break the cold, crisp salad greens into small-sized pieces and the orange slices into fourths. Combine with the ham, celery, and dressing in a large salad bowl. Toss lightly together. Garnish with thin slices of hard-cooked eggs. Serves six.

## COLESLAW

| | |
|---|---|
| 1 head red or white cabbage | Raw cauliflower |
| ½ cup mayonnaise or boiled dressing | Radishes |
| | Celery |
| Salt, pepper, cayenne | Carrots |
| Olives | Onion juice |

Shred the cabbage fine. Wash and put in a colander to drain; then chill in the coldest part of the refrigerator. When ready to serve, mix with the mayonnaise or boiled dressing, season, and put in a salad bowl for serving or directly on the salad plates. Serves four.

For special raw salad, pile the coleslaw in the center of a salad plate. In little piles around it, arrange strips of raw carrot marinated in onion juice; whole radishes with the peel cut back to the stem in four sections but left on; raw cauliflowerets; the smallest celery hearts; ripe or green olives. Add a little mayonnaise to the tips of the cauliflower.

## COLESLAW

| | |
|---|---|
| 2 cups shredded cabbage | ¼ teaspoon salt |
| ½ cup sour cream | ⅛ teaspoon pepper |
| 1 tablespoon vinegar | 1 tablespoon chopped pimiento |
| 1 tablespoon sugar | 1 tablespoon chopped onion |

Combine cabbage with the other ingredients. Chill in the refrigerator until ready to serve. Serves four.

## CUCUMBER CREAM SALAD

| | |
|---|---|
| ½ pint cream, whipped | 2 tablespoons gelatin |
| 1 tablespoon tarragon vinegar | Salt and cayenne |
| ½ cup finely cut peeled cucumbers | |

Dissolve gelatin in a little cold water and then add to whipped cream. Stir in the remaining ingredients. Pack either in four individual molds or one ring mold, and set on ice for several hours or in the coldest part of the automatic refrigerator. Garnish with strips of sweet red peppers, and serve on lettuce with sour cream or boiled dressing. Serves four.

## ENDIVE SALAD

Wash, drain, and chill the stalks of endive without cutting them. When ready to serve, cut down through the center and cover at once with a little French Dressing. Arrange on a small plate or as a garnish for a salad bowl. Endive is easily eaten with the fingers, and when only the root end is covered with the dressing each blade may be picked up.

## GARDEN SALAD

1 cucumber

½ cup radishes, sliced

3 red-ripe tomatoes

1 head lettuce

Sour Cream Dressing

Peel cucumber or score with the tines of a fork; slice thin and chill in the refrigerator while you prepare the other ingredients. Wash and slice the radishes, and chill; peel tomatoes and cut in quarters. Wash lettuce, drain, and arrange in salad bowl. Place the cut vegetables on this, and top with dressing. Serves four.

Add raw cauliflower broken in flowerets; also strips of green pepper, or finely minced raw spinach, or thin slivers of carrot.

## ORANGE CRANBERRY RELISH SALAD

2 oranges

1 lemon

2 apples

1 pound (4 cups) fresh cranberries

2½ cups sugar

Quarter unpeeled oranges, lemon, and apples; remove seeds and core, and put through the food chopper. Put cranberries through the chopper. Combine, add sugar, and blend. Let stand in a china or glass bowl or an enameled pan for a few hours. Use as a relish with cold meats or fowl, or on a salad plate. Enough to garnish ten or more plates.

## GRAPEFRUIT PERFECTION SALAD

1 envelope unflavored gelatin
⅛ cup water
2 cups Florida grapefruit sections
¼ cup vinegar

¼ cup sugar
½ teaspoon salt
1 pimiento, chopped
⅔ cup finely shredded cabbage
Lettuce

Mayonnaise

Sprinkle gelatin on water. Drain grapefruit, heat the juice, and add to the softened gelatin. Stir until dissolved. Add vinegar, sugar, and salt. Chill until syrupy. Fold in pimiento with grapefruit sections and cabbage. Put into six individual molds, chill until firm. Unmold on lettuce and serve with mayonnaise. Serves six.

## POTATO SALAD

6 cold boiled potatoes
4 tablespoons salad oil or melted butter
2 tablespoons vinegar

½ tablespoon salt
1 tablespoon onion juice
2 tablespoons minced parsley
Cayenne

1 teaspoon celery seed or poppy seed

Cut potatoes in half-inch cubes. Make a dressing of the other ingredients well mixed. Toss potatoes in dressing and let stand for twenty minutes. Drain and add a little mayonnaise or cream dressing. Sprinkle with minced chives and parsley. Serves four.

## GRAPEFRUIT STARTER SALAD

Halve Florida grapefruit; loosen sections by cutting around each with sharp knife along the membrane and skin; remove sections; cut out membrane. Combine sections with grated carrot and minced green pepper; moisten with French Dressing. Refill grapefruit shells; garnish with watercress. Serve a half to each person.

## ROMAINE AND GRAPEFRUIT SALAD

2 to 3 bunches of romaine,
    coarse outer leaves
    removed
2 grapefruit
French Dressing

Salad oil
Lemon juice
1 pimiento, or 1 sweet green
    pepper

Wash romaine and rinse in ice-cold water to make as crisp as possible. Drain and dry each leaf. Peel grapefruit close to the fruit; remove all white membrane between sections, so that each piece is clear. Let the pieces lie in lemon juice and oil (one part juice to three parts oil) to season. When ready to serve, dip each romaine leaf in Lemon French Dressing, and arrange in the salad bowl; place grapefruit sections in the center. Garnish with thin strips of pimiento or pepper. Pour Lemon French Dressing over all. Avocado makes a delicious addition to this salad. Cut the ripe pear in thin slivers, and arrange with the grapefruit in the bowl. Serves six.

## ROYAL SALAD

3 avocados
3 oranges, peeled and sectioned
2 Florida grapefruit, peeled
    and sectioned

2 bunches watercress
½ cup French Dressing

Cut avocados in half and remove seeds but do not peel. Fill hollows with alternate sections of orange and grapefruit. Place on a bed of crisp watercress. Serve with French Dressing. Makes six servings.

## SOUTHERN CHICKEN SALAD

2 cups diced cooked chicken
1 cup diced celery
2 tablespoons diced pimiento
2 tablespoons diced green pepper
¾ teaspoon salt
¼ teaspoon pepper
½ cup mayonnaise
Lettuce
2 cups Florida grapefruit sections
Stuffed olives

Mix lightly together chicken, celery, pimiento, green pepper, salt, pepper, and mayonnaise. Heap in a bed of crisp lettuce in the salad bowl. Surround with a ring of stuffed olives and grapefruit sections. Serves six.

## WESTERN FRUIT PLATE

On a bed of crisp, cold salad greens, alternate:

2 cups thin California orange slices, or sections
1 cup round unpeeled apple slices (sliced crosswise of the whole apple)

Around them group:

1 cup raisins                1 cup pitted dates

1 cup pitted prunes (soaked until tender, or briefly heated in a little water, then pitted and chilled)

The prunes and dates may be stuffed with nuts or cheese. Serve with any preferred dressing. Serves four.

## SPRING SALAD PLATTER

1 Florida grapefruit
2 oranges
1 bunch radishes

4 scallions
½ cup cottage cheese
½ cup mayonnaise

Lettuce

Peel and section grapefruit and oranges. Slice radishes; chop scallions. Combine scallions, cottage cheese, and one-fourth cup mayonnaise. Arrange lettuce on large salad platter; arrange grapefruit and orange sections and radish slices on lettuce. In center, pile cottage cheese; garnish with remaining mayonnaise. Serves four.

## TOSSED GREEN SALAD

2 endives, quartered
4 tomatoes, quartered
1 bunch watercress
1 cucumber, peeled and diced
1 bunch scallions

1 green pepper, sliced thin
1 bunch celery, diced
1 bunch radishes, sliced
Lettuce
French Dressing

Chill the washed vegetables in the refrigerator until ready to serve. Place in a large bowl. Add French Dressing to coat the top. Toss and mix lightly. Add a little more dressing to coat the rest of the mixture. Serve at once. Six servings.

## FRENCH DRESSING

¾ teaspoon salt
½ teaspoon dry mustard
½ teaspoon paprika
1 tablespoon sugar

2 tablespoons any favorite
    vinegar
2 tablespoons lemon juice
½ cup salad oil

Combine dry ingredients, add vinegar and lemon juice, and blend thoroughly. Add oil gradually and beat vigorously. Store in a bottle in the refrigerator and shake thoroughly before using.

## LEMON FRENCH DRESSING

½ cup lemon juice
½ cup salad oil
1 teaspoon each salt and
    paprika
2 tablespoons sugar or honey

Shake well together, and shake before serving. Makes one cup.
To make a sweet version of this for fruit salad plates, add one-half cup red jelly or an additional one-half cup honey.

## THICK FRENCH DRESSING

⅔ cup sugar
1 teaspoon celery seed
1 teaspoon salt
⅛ cup vinegar
⅛ cup lemon juice

1 teaspoon Worcestershire
    Sauce
⅛ cup chili sauce
1 tablespoon grated onion
1 cup oil

2 cloves

Combine ingredients, pour into bottle, and store in the refrigerator. Shake vigorously before serving.

## DRESSING FOR ALLIGATOR PEAR

Lemon juice, olive oil, and a little salt mixed make the classic dressing for alligator pear or avocado.
Here is another dressing which is delicious:

½ cup French Dressing
¼ cup mayonnaise
3 tablespoons chopped pimientos

1 tablespoon minced chives
2 hard-cooked eggs (chopped)
4 tablespoons chili sauce

Mix and serve very cold. Also delicious on shrimp and crab meat. Makes about two cups.

## CHIFFONADE DRESSING

1 tablespoon minced onion
2 tablespoons minced parsley
2 tablespoons minced celery

1 chopped hard-cooked egg
2 tablespoons minced green
          pepper

½ cup French Dressing

Mix smoothly. Serve on green salad.

## LEMON MAYONNAISE

1 egg or 2 egg yolks
¼ cup lemon juice
1 teaspoon mustard

1 teaspoon salt
1 tablespoon sugar
Dash of pepper or paprika

2 cups salad oil

Beat the eggs or egg yolks, two tablespoons lemon juice, and the seasonings thoroughly. Add the salad oil very slowly until the mixture begins to get very thick. Then add the remaining lemon juice. Gradually beat in the rest of the oil, and continue beating until well combined. Makes two and one-fourth cups.

## ORANGE AND LEMON SALAD DRESSING

3 tablespoons flour
2 tablespoons sugar
¾ teaspoon dry mustard
½ teaspoon salt

1 cup orange juice
2 egg yolks
1 tablespoon butter
¼ cup lemon juice

Mix the flour, sugar, mustard, and salt together thoroughly. Add the orange juice and the well-beaten egg yolks. Cook in a glass or enamel double boiler until thickened. Add the butter and lemon juice. Remove from the heat and chill. Makes one and one-half cups.

## HORSERADISH DRESSING

1 teaspoon salt
¼ teaspoon paprika
1 tablespoon horseradish
2 tablespoons chili sauce

1 tablespoon lemon juice, lime juice, or any vinegar
6 tablespoons salad oil
1 clove garlic

Mix all ingredients and blend well. Rub salad bowl with garlic. Toss greens in it with a spoonful or two of dressing. Pour the rest of the dressing over, and serve. Makes a little less than one cup.

## RAVIGOTE MAYONNAISE

2 tablespoons cooked spinach, finely chopped
1 tablespoon capers
½ shallot, finely chopped

3 anchovies
⅓ cup parsley, finely chopped
½ cup watercress, finely chopped

1 cup mayonnaise

Pound in mortar or mix in bowl thoroughly until all the greens are finely pulverized and mixture is smooth. Put through sieve. Then add to the mayonnaise. Have cold for serving. About two cups.

## RUSSIAN SALAD DRESSING

½ cup mayonnaise
½ teaspoon English mustard
3 tablespoons chili sauce
2 tablespoons chopped green pepper

1 tablespoon tarragon vinegar
1 tablespoon minced chives or onion
1 tablespoon piccalilli

Mix, chill, and serve on lettuce hearts or endive, on crab meat or shrimp. About one cup.

## ROMAINE SALAD DRESSING

1 tablespoon heavy mayonnaise
1 dessertspoon chili sauce
½ teaspoon Escoffier Sauce
    Diable

Juice of ½ lemon
Salt, pepper, paprika
½ teaspoon chopped chives or
    finely minced onion

Mix and chill for crisp greens on salad plates. Enough for two or three.

## SOUR CREAM DRESSING

¾ cup sour cream
¼ cup lemon juice
½ teaspoon salt

1 pimiento, cut fine
1 tablespoon sugar
1 teaspoon minced chives

Mix ingredients and chill. Makes one and one-fourth cups.

## DRESSING FOR FRUIT PLATE

½ cup orange juice
3 tablespoons lemon juice

½ teaspoon salt
¼ teaspoon paprika

Few grains nutmeg

Shake well or stir just before serving. Not quite one cup.

## APPLE CUSTARD

4 large apples
4 tablespoons sugar
1 saltspoon salt

1 tablespoon butter
1 tablespoon powdered sugar
1 cup milk

4 eggs, yolks and whites separated

Core apples, and bake until tender. Scoop out the flesh while hot. Add sugar, butter, milk, and beaten yolks of eggs, beating well as each ingredient is added. Turn the mixture into a baking dish, and bake slowly (300 degrees F.) twenty-five minutes. Beat whites of eggs stiffly. Add one tablespoon powdered sugar. Heap this meringue over the custard in the baking dish, and brown in the oven. Serve cool with cream flavored with nutmeg or a few drops of essence of lemon. Serves four or five.

## APPLE DELICIOUS

8 apples
1½ tablespoons butter

½ cup sugar
½ cup bread crumbs

½ cup chopped nuts

Peel and core the apples. Mix bread crumbs, nuts, and sugar. Melt the butter. Roll the apples first in the butter, and then in the nut mixture. Place in a buttered baking dish; put a few table-spoons of water in the bottom. Bake in a hot oven (425 degrees F.) till a light brown. Serve cold with whipped cream or plain cream. Serves eight.

## BAKED APPLES

Core and pare apples, fill centers with butter and sugar, a leaf or two of fresh mint, and a grating of lemon peel. Dust cinnamon and nutmeg sparingly over all. Place in casserole. Put a few tablespoons of water in the bottom of the dish. Bake in a hot oven until tender (325 degrees F). Serve cool with cream and sugar, or plain. Bake one for each serving.

## OHIO APPLE PUDDING

6 medium-sized apples
1 tablespoon sugar
1 cup butter
1 cup brown sugar
2 cups flour

Peel and slice apples into the casserole as for a deep dish pie. Add the tablespoon of sugar. Make crust of butter, brown sugar, and flour rubbed and mixed together. Cover the dish. Bake in a moderate oven (375 degrees F.) until the crust is taffy brown. Serve hot with cream or top milk. Serves six.

## SWEDISH APPLE PUDDING

2½ pounds apples
⅔ cup sugar
½ cup water
½ loaf day-old pumpernickel, crumbed, or 2 cups crumbs
½ cup butter

Peel apples, core, and cut into thin slices. Cook to a pulp with sugar and water. Grate the pumpernickel or put through a mincer, and brown lightly in almost all of the butter. Spread buttered casserole with crumbs, then a layer of apples, and crumbs and apples repeated until all are used. Make the top layer of crumbs. Dot on top with butter. Bake in a moderate oven (375 degrees F.) thirty minutes. Serve hot or cold with cream or vanilla sauce. Serves six.

## BAKED BANANAS

6 ripe bananas, peeled and laid in a baking dish
Grated lemon or orange peel
Brown sugar

*Put into a bowl:*

3 tablespoons butter
7 tablespoons sugar

3 tablespoons lemon juice
1 tablespoon orange juice
½ glass sherry

Mix these and let stand in a bowl set over hot water until the butter is melted. Then pour the mixture over the bananas. Sprinkle lightly with brown sugar and grated peel of one orange.

Bake in a hot oven (400 degrees F.) thirty minutes, basting frequently with the juices in the pan. Serve as an entrée, or with game or fowl, or as a dessert. Serves six.

## BAKED BANANAS

6 bananas
2 tablespoons melted butter
3 tablespoons lemon juice

⅓ cup brown, or maple sugar, or honey

Remove skins from bananas, cut in halves lengthwise, and place in a shallow baking dish. Mix the melted butter, sugar, and lemon juice, and pour over the bananas. Bake in a slow oven (250 degrees F.) thirty minutes. Serve sprinkled with freshly grated coconut, or plain. Serves six.

## BAKED PEACHES

6 large ripe peaches, or canned peaches
¼ cup brown, or maple sugar, or honey

1 tablespoon butter
Lemon juice
Cinnamon

Cut the peaches in half, remove the stones. Fill each cavity with one teaspoon sugar or a little honey, about one-fourth teaspoon butter, a few drops lemon juice, and a sprinkle of cinnamon. Bake in a shallow casserole in a moderate oven (275 degrees F.) twenty minutes. If not very juicy, add a few spoonfuls of hot water to the casserole. Serve with cream. Serves six.

## BAKED PEARS

Follow recipe for Baked Peaches; use brown sugar; cover bottom of the casserole with hot water, or hot water and any fruit juice. Bake as for peaches, and serve with cream.

## BAKED QUINCES

Wash, core, and parboil. Then bake as for peaches. Serve warm with cream or with custard sauce.

## BANANA BETTY

¼ cup melted butter          ¾ cup brown sugar
2 cups bread crumbs          6 bananas
1 teaspoon cinnamon          3 tablespoons lemon juice
                    1½ cups milk

Moisten bread crumbs in melted butter and lemon juice, combine with sugar and cinnamon. Slice three bananas in the bottom of a buttered baking dish, sprinkle with half the bread crumb mixture. Repeat with bananas and crumbs. Pour milk over, and bake in a moderate oven (350 degrees F.) thirty minutes. Serve with cream. Serves six.

## BANANA PUDDING

Peel and cut bananas very thin; put a layer in the bottom of a well-buttered baking dish; cover with a layer of buttered crumbs. Continue with alternate layers of banana and crumbs until the dish is nearly full.

Then pour this over the fruit:

4 eggs                       1 cup sugar
1½ cups milk                 1 teaspoon vanilla

Beat the eggs separately, the whites to stiffness; add the sugar to the yolks, add vanilla, beat in the whites; then pour over the fruit and set the casserole in a pan of hot water. Bake till the custard is firm in a moderate oven (300 degrees F.) about twenty-five minutes. A spoonful or two of sherry added to the custard gives added flavor which is liked by most people. Serves six.

## CALIFORNIA BAKED BANANAS

| 1 pound dried apricots | 4 peeled bananas |
|---|---|
| | Sugar |

Soak apricots overnight; cook till tender in enough water to cover, adding enough sugar to sweeten. When tender, rub through a sieve. Place the thick purée in a buttered baking dish, lay the peeled bananas cut in halves in this, and bake fifteen minutes in a moderate oven (375 degrees F.). Serve cold with or without cream. Serves four.

## BERRY LOAF

| 1 quart fresh berries (raspberries are best) | Sugar |
|---|---|
| | 1 small loaf cake |

Boil the berries with sufficient sugar and a little water to make a thick stew. Cut the crust from the loaf cake; place in a serving dish, and pour the berries over the cake. Let cool, basting the loaf from time to time with the syrup so as to penetrate the cake thoroughly. Serve with fresh cream, plain or whipped. Serves four to six.

## BUTTERSCOTCH BREAD PUDDING

| ¾ cup brown sugar | ¼ teaspoon salt |
|---|---|
| 2 tablespoons butter | 1½ cups bread-and-butter cubes |
| 2 cups milk | ½ teaspoon vanilla |
| 2 eggs, beaten separately | ¼ cup brown sugar for meringue |

Put butter and sugar in the top of a metal double boiler. Stir this over the fire until it begins to boil. Let boil one minute, stirring constantly, being very careful that it does not burn. The sugar should become slightly caramelized. Add milk, and place over hot water. When milk is scalded, add slowly to the two egg yolks beaten with the salt.

Butter a casserole. Put in the buttered bread cubes, pour mixture over them, and cook in a moderate oven (350 degrees F.) until firm.

Beat whites of eggs until stiff, fold in one-fourth cup brown sugar, add one-half teaspoon vanilla. Pile on top of pudding. Return to the oven for about eight minutes. Turn oven down to 275 degrees F. for the meringue. Serves four to five.

## CARAMEL BREAD PUDDING

½ cup sugar
2 cups scalded milk
2 cups bread crumbs

1 egg
¼ teaspoon salt
½ teaspoon vanilla

Caramelize sugar by melting it over moderate heat in a heavy shallow pan, stirring constantly. Then add to the scalded milk. When the sugar has dissolved, add the bread crumbs, beaten egg, salt, and vanilla. Mix and turn into a small buttered baking dish. Bake in a moderate oven (350 degrees F.) one hour. Serve with milk or cream. Serves four.

## CHERRIES MOROCCO

1 can black pitted cherries
1 cup juice from the cherries

3 tablespoons brandy
2 tablespoons kirsch

Heat the cherries in a chafing dish in as much of the juice as you want. Add the brandy to the hot cherries and juice in the dish, and set afire; when the flames have gone down, add the kirsch. Serve with vanilla ice cream, or with spongecake or angel cake. Enough for four to six servings.

## BAKED CHOCOLATE CUSTARD

2 squares unsweetened choco-
    late
4 cups milk

4 eggs, slightly beaten
⅓ cup sugar
¼ teaspoon salt
1 teaspoon vanilla

Add chocolate to milk, and heat in double boiler. When chocolate is melted, beat with rotary egg beater until blended. Combine eggs, sugar, and salt; add chocolate mixture gradually, stirring until sugar is dissolved. Add vanilla, and pour into custard cups. Place in a pan of hot water, and bake in slow oven (325 degrees F.) forty-five minutes, or until knife inserted comes out clean. (Water in pan should not reach boiling temperature.) Chill. Top with cream and a dash of cinnamon, or unmold and serve with cream, if desired. Serves eight to ten.

## CHOCOLATE SOUFFLÉ

2 squares unsweetened choco-
    late
2 cups milk
½ cup sugar
⅓ cup flour

½ teaspoon salt
2 tablespoons butter
1 teaspoon vanilla
4 egg yolks, beaten until thick
    and lemon-colored

4 egg whites, stiffly beaten

The baking dish should first be buttered and dusted with granulated sugar to give interesting finish and texture.

Add chocolate to the milk and heat in a double boiler. When chocolate is melted, beat with rotary beater until blended. Combine sugar, flour, and salt; add a small amount of chocolate mixture, stirring until smooth; return to the double boiler and cook until thickened, stirring constantly; then continue cooking five minutes, stirring occasionally. Add butter and vanilla; cool slightly while beating eggs. Add egg yolks and mix well. Fold into egg whites. Turn into greased baking dish. Place in pan of hot water, and bake in moderate oven (350 degrees F.) one hour, or until soufflé is firm. Serve immediately with Chocolate Mint Sauce or with cream. Serves eight.

## CHOCOLATE MINT CREAM

Use recipe for Chocolate Velvet Cream (below). Dissolve gelatin as directed. Add only two cups gelatin mixture to melted chocolate. Pour one-half of chocolate mixture into large mold or individual molds, and chill until firm. Place remaining chocolate mixture over lukewarm water until ready to mold.

To the remaining plain gelatin mixture, add a few drops of peppermint extract and green coloring to tint a delicate green. Chill until cold and syrupy. Place in bowl of cracked ice or ice water, and whip with rotary egg beater until thickened. Turn into mold over the firm chocolate layer, and chill until firm. Top with remaining chocolate mixture. Chill until firm. Serve plain or with whipped cream.

## CHOCOLATE VELVET CREAM

| | |
|---|---|
| 2 squares unsweetened chocolate | 1¼ cups milk, scalded |
| | ½ cup sugar |
| 1 tablespoon granulated gelatin | ⅛ teaspoon salt |
| ¼ cup milk | 1 cup light cream |
| ¾ teaspoon vanilla | |

Melt chocolate in the top of a double boiler. Soak gelatin for five minutes in one-fourth cup of milk. Add scalded milk, sugar, and salt, and stir until gelatin is dissolved; add cream. Pour gelatin mixture slowly into melted chocolate, beating with rotary egg beater until blended; then cook five minutes. Remove from boil, ing water and add vanilla. Chill until cold and syrupy. Place in bowl of cracked ice or ice water, and whip with rotary egg beater until thickened. Turn into mold. Chill until firm. Serve plain or with whipped cream. Serves six.

This pudding may also be put in individual molds or turned into sherbet glasses.

## FLOATING ISLAND

| | |
|---|---|
| 3 egg yolks | 2 cups scalded milk |
| ¼ cup sugar | ½ teaspoon vanilla |
| ⅛ teaspoon salt | 3 egg whites |
| | 3 tablespoons sugar |

Beat egg yolks slightly, add sugar and salt. Add hot milk, stirring constantly. Cook over hot water and continue stirring until mixture thickens. Remove from fire, add vanilla, and chill in the refrigerator. Beat egg whites, add sugar and flavoring. Pile by spoonfuls on the chilled custard. Serves six.

## COCONUT BREAD PUDDING

| | |
|---|---|
| 3 eggs, beaten | 1½ cups orange juice |
| 1⅛ cups sugar | 4 cups cubes day-old bread |
| ¼ teaspoon salt | ¼ cup grated coconut |
| | 2 tablespoons raisins |

Combine eggs, sugar, salt, and orange juice. Pour over the bread. Stir in the raisins and coconut. Bake in a buttered casserole in a moderate oven (350 degrees F.) about thirty minutes, or until set. Increase the oven heat to hot (450 degrees F.) to brown the peaks of the pudding. Serve with orange sauce. Serves six.

### SAUCE

| | |
|---|---|
| 1 tablespoon cornstarch | 1 cup orange juice |
| ½ cup sugar | 1 tablespoon lemon juice |
| 1 teaspoon grated orange peel | 2 tablespoons butter |

Mix cornstarch, sugar, peel, and juice. Boil five minutes in a glass or enamel saucepan. Remove from the fire. Add lemon juice and butter. Serve hot. This makes enough for four to six servings —six if you believe in small amounts of sauce. I like lots.

## GRAPEFRUIT APPLE CRISP

| | |
|---|---|
| 2 Florida grapefruit, sectioned | 1 teaspoon cinnamon |
| 3 apples, peeled and sliced thin | 1 cup honey |
| 2 tablespoons water | ⅔ cup sifted flour |
| ½ cup butter | |

Fill a casserole with grapefruit sections, apples, the water, and cinnamon. Blend remaining ingredients to a crumbly consistency. Spread over top of grapefruit and apples, and bake uncovered in moderate oven (375 degrees F.) forty-five minutes. Serve hot or cold with hard sauce or cream. Serves six.

## FLORIDA GRAPEFRUIT SOUFFLÉ

| | |
|---|---|
| ½ cup grapefruit sections diced | ½ cup sugar |
| 4 tablespoons butter | 3 tablespoons orange juice |
| 4 tablespoons flour | Grated rind 1 orange |
| 1 cup milk | 1 tablespoon lemon juice |
| 4 egg yolks, well beaten | 4 egg whites |

With a sharp knife, cut a thick layer off the top and bottom of a grapefruit; peel around fruit deep enough to remove all white membrane; cut on either side of each dividing membrane and remove meat, section by section. Cut each section into three pieces.

Melt butter, blend in flour, add milk, stirring constantly, and cook until thickened. Add well-beaten egg yolks. Add sugar, orange juice and rind, then the grapefruit sections and lemon juice. Beat egg whites stiff and carefully fold into the mixture. Pour into buttered baking dish, set in a pan of hot water, and bake in a slow oven (325 degrees F.) about one hour. Serve immediately. Serves four to five.

## LEMON CRUMB PUDDING

2 cups scalded milk
2 cups dry bread crumbs
¼ teaspoon salt
¼ cup sugar

1 egg, well beaten
Grated rind 1 lemon
3 tablespoons lemon juice
1 tablespoon melted butter

Pour scalded milk over fine bread crumbs and add remaining ingredients. Mix and pour into a shallow greased baking dish. Bake in a moderate oven (325 degrees F.) forty-five minutes. Serve hot with lemon sauce or cream or top milk. Serves four to six.

## MELON FILLED WITH FRUIT

1 large very fine honeydew melon
2 cups fine big blueberries
2 cups fresh red raspberries

2 cups quartered and sliced bananas
2 tablespoons powdered sugar
½ cup rum or kirsch

Wash the melon and remove a thin slice from the bottom, so it will set steadily on the tray. Remove the top of the melon, about one and one-half inches deep, making the opening three to four inches in diameter. Pour out the liquid and carefully remove the seeds with a silver spoon. Scoop out the melon meat but do not break the shell. Cut melon meat in balls and mix with the cleaned berries and lastly the sliced bananas (which should be prepared only when ready to mix with the other fruits). Sprinkle powdered sugar over the fruit; add the rum or kirsch and mix lightly. Chill thoroughly. Chill melon also and at serving time fill the melon with the fruit mixture. Replace the top piece, or cover with clean grape leaves. Serve from the melon into dessert dishes or large fruit cups. Serves eight.

## ORANGE BAVARIAN

| | |
|---|---|
| 1 tablespoon gelatin | ⅔ cup evaporated milk or whipping cream, thoroughly chilled |
| 1½ cups orange juice | |
| ½ cup sugar | |
| 1 tablespoon lemon juice | |

Soften gelatin in one-fourth cup orange juice and liquefy over hot water. Combine the remaining one and one-fourth cups orange juice with sugar. Add gelatin and set in cold place, stirring occasionally to dissolve the sugar. When the mixture is set to a soft jelly, whip the milk or cream stiff. Fold in lemon juice, then the orange-gelatin mixture. Pour into a mold to set. Serves eight.

## FILLED PINEAPPLE

| | |
|---|---|
| 1 fine pineapple | Few muscatel grapes |
| Sugar | 2 small very ripe peaches |
| ½ cup strawberries | Mint jelly |

Cut off the top of the pineapple, retaining tips and all as a lid. Scoop out the contents of the pineapple and cut in small cubes, leaving only the rind with a thin inside layer of fruit pulp. Put the pineapple cubes into a bowl with the other fruits cut in small pieces. Mix all with a few spoonfuls of any favorite jelly (mint is very good with the pineapple flavor) and fill the pineapple shell.

Set on the ice to make very cold, or in the coldest part of the refrigerator. Just before taking to the table, replace the top of the pineapple. Four servings.

## ORANGE SOUFFLÉ WITH CUSTARD

4 egg whites                    4 tablespoons sugar
4 tablespoons orange marmalade

Fold the sugar slowly into stiffly beaten egg whites and gradually fold in the marmalade. Pour into the top part of a double boiler and place over boiling water. Cover and cook fifty minutes. Serve hot with the custard. Decorate with slices of unpeeled orange. Serves six.

### CUSTARD

4 egg yolks                     ¼ teaspoon salt
⅓ cup sugar                     1 cup orange juice
1 tablespoon cornstarch         1 cup cream or top milk
1 teaspoon grated orange peel

Add sugar, cornstarch, salt, juice, and cream or milk to the well-beaten egg yolks. Cook in a glass or enamel double boiler until thickened or until the mixture coats a spoon. Add grated orange peel. Cool quickly. Serve as a simple dessert or as sauce with the soufflé above.

## RASPBERRY SLUMP

1 quart raspberries             1½ teaspoons baking powder
1½ cups sugar                   ¼ cup sugar or honey
1 cup flour                     2 tablespoons melted butter
½ teaspoon salt                 ½ cup milk

Wash berries and put in a buttered baking dish; sprinkle with sugar. Make a smooth batter of the remaining ingredients and pour over the berries. Bake in a moderate oven (325 degrees **F.**) forty-five minutes. Serves six.

Substitute blackberries, boysenberries, blueberries, currants, or gooseberries, using more sugar for the last two unless they are very ripe and very sweet.

## RICE CUSTARD, BRAZILIAN

| | |
|---|---|
| 3 eggs | 2 cups hot milk |
| ½ cup sugar | 1 cup cooked rice |
| Few grains salt | 1 teaspoon vanilla |

½ cup thinly sliced Brazil nuts

Beat eggs slightly; add sugar and salt. Add milk gradually. Add rice, vanilla, and Brazil nuts. Pour into a baking dish; place in a pan of hot water. Bake in moderate oven (350 degrees **F.**) about forty-five minutes. Chill. Serves six.

## OLD-FASHIONED STRAWBERRY SHORTCAKE

| | |
|---|---|
| 2½ cups flour | 2½ teaspoons baking powder |
| ½ teaspoon salt | Milk |
| ½ cup butter | 1 quart red-ripe perfect berries |
| 2 tablespoons melted butter | Sugar |

Hull, wash, and pick over the berries, discarding any under-ripe or spoiled ones. Cover with sugar and let stand one hour or longer.

Sift flour, salt, and baking powder together twice, then work in the butter with two spatulas or with the fingers. Add enough milk to make a soft dough. Roll out the dough and put into a small layer-cake pan. Bake in a hot oven (425 degrees **F.**) fifteen minutes. Split the cake in half while warm and remove a little of the soft inside. Brush the bottom layer with melted butter; pile this half with berries; place the other half on top and sprinkle with powdered sugar thickly. Garnish the top with fine whole berries. Serve with plain heavy cream. Serves six.

## STRAWBERRY-RASPBERRY DESSERT

2 boxes strawberries
2 boxes red raspberries

2 cups heavy cream
½ cup water

Wash all the berries, mash together thoroughly. Use a strainer to strain off the excess juice. Add a half cup water, then mix in the whipped cream. Turn into a mold; cover tightly and pack down in ice and salt for four to five hours. Raspberry ice will form on top, leaving a delicately flavored cream below it. Serves eight to ten.

## SOUTHERN SOUFFLÉ

1 pound eating apples
1 cup cream

Wild strawberry jam
½ cup sugar

3 eggs, well beaten

Peel and cut the apples into eighths; place sliced apples in a casserole or soufflé mold. Add two or three tablespoons of water. Bake in a moderate oven (375 degrees F.) about twenty minutes. When about three-fourths cooked, pour off any excessive juice, and dot with the jam; pour over this the cream to which the sugar and well-beaten eggs have been added. Finish cooking in the oven until well set. Serve from the casserole with cream or whipped cream. Serves four to six.

## HOT WATER PIE CRUST

¼ cup boiling water
½ cup butter

1½ cups flour
⅛ teaspoon baking powder

1⅛ teaspoons salt

Pour boiling water over the butter and beat with a fork until it becomes a smooth liquid. Sift flour, baking powder, and salt together, and then sift into the liquid. Stir together, chill, and roll out. Mixture keeps well in the refrigerator. Enough for a two-crust eight-inch pie.

## ICE WATER PIE CRUST

2 cups pastry flour  
½ teaspoon salt  
½ cup lard  
1 cup butter  
Ice-cold water

Mix flour and salt together, sift, and then cut lard and butter into the flour with two knives. Add enough water to make the particles hold together. Handle quickly, rolling or patting into shape on a pie plate. This makes a top and bottom crust for an eight-inch pie.

## FLAKY PASTRY

1½ cups sifted flour  
½ teaspoon salt  
⅔ cup shortening  
¼ cup ice water

Sift flour and salt, add shortening, and chop into the dry ingredients with pastry knife or two spatulas. Add ice water and form dough; turn onto floured board and roll out thin, fold together into three layers, roll out again. Repeat folding and rolling once more. Keep cold, chilling between rollings if possible. One double-crust eight-inch pie.

## APPLE PIE

Pastry  
Cooking apples  
Sugar  
Grated rind 1 lemon  
Cinnamon or nutmeg

Peel, quarter, and core apples, then cut into slices. Line pie dish with pastry, half fill it with apples, sprinkling with sugar, spice, and lemon rind. Cover with more apples, moisten pastry at edge of plate, and cover with top crust, pressing the edges firmly together, using thumb and forefinger to make a ruffled edge, if you like.

Very juicy apples require no water; others need a spoonful or two added. Make one or two slits in the top pastry crust to allow escape of steam. Bake forty-five minutes to one hour in a hot oven (425 degrees F.) for the first fifteen minutes, then reduce to 350 to 375 degrees.

For a cheese crust (to be added to pie served when no other cheese is in the menu) add two tablespoons grated cheese to each crust when rolling, and sprinkle finely grated cheese over the apples before putting the crust on. Bake as for plain crust.

## APPLE TARTS

Bake as for apple pie, using small tart pans.

## BERRY TARTS

In using fresh or canned berries, add more sugar than is required for apples, unless canned berries are already sweetened. Do not add water to berry mixtures.

## ANGEL PIE

### CRUST

4 egg whites                      ¾ cup sugar
¼ teaspoon cream of tartar

Beat egg whites until frothy and add cream of tartar. Gradually add sugar and continue beating until stiff. Spread in a nine-inch ungreased pie plate. Bake one hour in a slow oven (300 degrees F.). Let cool.

**FILLING**

4 egg yolks
½ cup sugar
Few grains salt
2 tablespoons orange juice

1 tablespoon lemon juice
1 teaspoon grated lemon peel
1 teaspoon grated orange peel
1 cup cream, whipped

2 tablespoons powdered sugar

Beat egg yolks, sugar, salt, orange and lemon juice and peel in upper part of a glass or enamel double boiler. Place over hot water. Stir and cook until thick. Whip cream with powdered sugar, and spread half of it over the crust. Spread this with the filling, and then cover with the remaining whipped cream. Chill in the refrigerator for twelve to twenty-four hours.

## MARVEL CHOCOLATE PIE

2 squares unsweetened chocolate
1 cup milk
1 tablespoon granulated gelatin
½ cup sugar

¼ teaspoon salt
3 egg yolks, slightly beaten
½ teaspoon vanilla
3 egg whites, stiffly beaten
1 baked 9-inch pie shell

Add chocolate to milk, and heat in double boiler. When chocolate is melted, beat with rotary egg beater until blended. Combine gelatin, sugar, and salt; mix thoroughly and add to chocolate mixture. Stir until sugar and gelatin are dissolved. Add gradually to egg yolks, and blend. Add vanilla, and chill. When slightly thickened, beat with rotary egg beater until light and foamy. Fold into egg whites. Turn into cold pie shell, and chill until firm.

## CHOCOLATE-CRESTED CUSTARD PIE

Pastry
4 eggs, slightly beaten
¼ cup sugar
¼ teaspoon salt
3 cups milk

1 teaspoon vanilla
2 tablespoons sugar
1 square unsweetened chocolate, melted
2 tablespoons hot water

Line a deep nine-inch pie plate with pastry, rolled one-eighth inch thick, allowing pastry to extend one inch beyond edge. Fold edge back to form standing rim; flute with fingers. Combine eggs, sugar, salt, milk, and vanilla. Pour into pie shell. Bake in hot oven (450 degrees F.) twenty minutes; then decrease heat to moderate (350 degrees F.) and bake ten to fifteen minutes longer, or until knife inserted comes out clean.

Add sugar to chocolate; then add water, one tablespoon at a time, stirring until blended. Pour over pie filling, and bake in slow oven (300 degrees F.) seven to ten minutes, or until set. Cool.

### HONEY OR CORN SYRUP SUBSTITUTED FOR SUGAR IN CAKE-MAKING

In cake-making, if corn syrup or honey is substituted for all or part of the sugar, add gradually to the creamed shortening or to the shortening and sugar mixture. Beat thoroughly after each addition. Then add one-fourth of the flour before adding the eggs. This helps to prevent the batter from curdling. This makes for smoothness in the batter, and the cake will be of fine texture, fine appearance, and good volume.

The resulting sweetness is not the same as when sugar is used; generally corn syrup or honey may be substituted for half the sugar, if one-fourth less liquid is used.

## CHOCOLATE-COVERED SUGARLESS CAKE

| | |
|---|---|
| 1¾ cups sifted cake flour | 1 cup light corn syrup |
| 1¾ teaspoons baking powder | 2 egg yolks, unbeaten |
| ¼ teaspoon salt | ⅓ cup milk |
| ⅓ cup butter or other shortening | 1½ teaspoons vanilla |
| 1½ teaspoons grated orange rind | 2 egg whites |

Sift flour once, measure, add baking powder and salt, and sift together three times. Cream shortening with orange rind; add syrup very gradually by tablespoons at first, beating very hard after each addition to keep mixture thick. Add one-fourth of flour, and beat until smooth and well blended. Add egg yolks one at a time, beating well after each. Add remaining flour in thirds, alternately with milk in halves, beating very well after each addition. For best results, beat cake very well at each stage of mixing. Add vanilla, and beat mixture well again.

Beat egg whites until they will hold up in moist peaks. Stir quickly but thoroughly into batter. Bake in two greased eight-inch layer pans in moderate oven (375 degrees F.) twenty minutes, or until done. Cover with frosting.

## CHOCOLATE MARBLE CAKE

| | |
|---|---|
| 1 square unsweetened chocolate, melted | 6 tablespoons butter or other shortening |
| 1 tablespoon sugar | 1 cup sugar (substitute corn syrup or honey for half of sugar; use ½ cup each; decrease milk to ½ cup) |
| 2 tablespoons hot water | |
| ¼ teaspoon soda | |
| 2 cups sifted cake flour | |
| 2 teaspoons baking powder | ¾ cup milk |
| ¼ teaspoon salt | 1 teaspoon vanilla |
| 3 egg whites | |

To melted chocolate, add one tablespoon sugar, hot water, and soda and blend. Cool.

Sift flour once, measure, add baking powder and salt, and sift together three times. Cream shortening, add one cup sugar gradually, and cream together until light and fluffy. Add flour alternately with milk, a small amount at a time, beating after each addition until smooth. Add vanilla. Beat egg whites until they will hold up in moist peaks. Stir quickly but thoroughly into cake batter.

Add chocolate mixture to one-third of batter. Put by table-spoons into two greased eight-inch layer pans, alternating light and dark mixtures. Then with knife cut carefully through batter once in a wide zigzag course. Bake in moderate oven (375 degrees F.) twenty-five minutes, or until done. Spread Hungarian Chocolate Frosting between layers and on top and sides of cake.

## MARBLE LOAF CAKE

Use recipe for Chocolate Marble Cake (above), decreasing milk to two-thirds cup. Bake in greased pan, nine-by-five-by-three inches, in moderate oven (350 degrees F.) one hour, or until done. Spread with Chocolate Frosting or Cocoa Frosting, if desired.

## CHOCOLATE PEPPERMINT CAKE

2 cups sifted cake flour
1 teaspoon soda
½ teaspoon salt
⅓ cup butter or other shortening
1¼ cups sugar

1 egg, unbeaten
3 squares unsweetened chocolate, melted
1 teaspoon vanilla
½ cup sour cream
1 cup sweet milk

Sift flour once, measure, add soda and salt, and sift together three times. Cream shortening, add sugar gradually, and cream together well. Add egg, and beat very thoroughly. Add chocolate and vanilla; blend. Add about one-fourth of flour, and beat well; then add sour cream, and beat thoroughly. Add remaining flour in fourths, alternately with milk in thirds, beating after each addition until smooth. Turn quickly into two greased nine-inch layer pans and bake in moderate oven (350 degrees F.) twenty-five to thirty minutes. Spread Peppermint Frosting between layers and on top and sides of cake.

## DEVIL'S FOOD CAKE

2 cups sifted cake flour
1 teaspoon soda
¼ teaspoon salt
½ cup butter or other shortening
1 cup milk
1 teaspoon vanilla

1¼ cups sugar (or substitute corn syrup or honey for half of sugar. Use ⅖ cup of each, and decrease milk to ¾ cup)
2 eggs or 3 egg yolks, unbeaten
2 to 3 squares unsweetened chocolate, melted

Sift flour once, measure, add soda and salt, and sift together three times. Cream shortening, add sugar gradually, and cream together until light and fluffy. Add eggs one at a time, beating well after each; then add chocolate, and blend. Add flour alternately with milk, a small amount at a time, beating after each addition until smooth. Add vanilla. Bake in two greased deep nine-inch layer pans or three greased eight-inch layer pans in moderate oven (350 degrees F.) twenty-five minutes, or until done. Spread Fluffy Seven Minute Frosting or Peppermint Frosting between layers and on the top and sides.

## LOW-SUGAR CHOCOLATE CAKE

1¾ cups sifted cake flour
1½ teaspoons soda
½ teaspoon salt
½ cup butter or other shortening
4 tablespoons sugar

1 cup corn syrup
2 egg yolks, unbeaten
2 squares unsweetened chocolate, melted
⅔ cup milk
1 teaspoon vanilla

2 egg whites

Sift flour once, measure, add soda and salt, and sift together three times. Cream shortening, add sugar, and cream well. Add syrup very gradually by tablespoons at first, beating very hard after each addition to keep mixture thick. Then add one-fourth of flour, and beat until smooth and well blended. Add egg yolks one at a time, beating well after each. Add chocolate, and blend. Add remaining flour in thirds, alternately with milk in halves, beating very well after each addition. Add vanilla, and beat the mixture well again.

Beat egg whites until they will hold up in moist peaks. Stir quickly but thoroughly into batter. Bake in two greased nine-inch layer pans in moderate oven (350 degrees F.) twenty-five minutes, or until done. Spread Fluffy Seven Minute Frosting between layers and on top and sides of cake.

Double this recipe to make three ten-inch-layer party cake.

## NEW ORLEANS FUDGE LOAF

1¾ cups sifted cake flour
1¾ teaspoons baking powder
½ teaspoon salt
1 teaspoon vanilla
1 egg, well beaten
2 squares unsweetened chocolate, melted
¾ cup milk

½ cup butter or other shortening
1 cup sugar (or substitute corn syrup or honey for half of sugar, using ½ cup of each; decrease milk to ½ cup plus 1 tablespoon)

Sift flour once, measure, add baking powder and salt, and sift together three times. Cream shortening, add sugar gradually, and cream together until light and fluffy. Add egg, and beat well; then add chocolate, and blend. Add flour alternately with milk, a small amount at a time, beating after each addition until smooth. Add vanilla. Bake in greased pan, eight-by-eight-by-two inches, in slow oven (325 degrees F.) one hour, or until done.

Spread Fluffy Seven Minute Frosting on top and sides of cake. When frosting is set, pour chocolate coating over cake, letting it run down on sides. Keep cake in a cool place until chocolate becomes firm.

## HICKORY NUT CAKE

¾ cup butter
1½ cups sugar
¾ cup liquid, water and milk mixed

2½ cups flour
1 teaspoon baking powder
2 cups chopped hickory nuts
5 egg whites

Cream the butter and sugar, and add liquid alternately with the mixed and sifted flour and baking powder. Add the stiffly beaten egg whites and fold in quickly, then add nuts. Turn at once into pound-cake tin, lined with waxed paper which has been greased. Bake in moderate oven (325 degrees F.) forty-five minutes. Turn on cake rack to cool. Serve iced or plain.

## ORANGE SPONGECAKE

5 egg yolks
1¼ cups sugar
½ cup orange juice
½ cup water
2 cups sifted cake flour

2 teaspoons baking powder
⅛ teaspoon salt
1 tablespoon grated orange peel
5 egg whites

Beat egg yolks, sugar, and orange juice for ten minutes with a rotary hand or electric beater. Add water, and beat two minutes. Add flour sifted with baking powder and salt. Beat about one minute, or only until the dry ingredients have been quickly and thoroughly blended into the mixture. Fold in the grated peel and egg whites beaten stiff but not dry. Bake in a nine-inch ungreased tube pan in a moderate oven (350 degrees F.) seventy

minutes. Invert the pan on a cake rack until the cake is cold.
Remove. Serve as plain spongecake, or divide into layers by cutting crosswise in three equal layers and spreading with orange
topping.

### ORANGE TOPPING

¼ cup cold water

1 tablespoon gelatin

4 egg yolks

¾ cup sugar

1 cup orange juice

1 teaspoon grated orange peel

4 egg whites

¼ cup sugar

Soften gelatin in water. Cook egg yolks, sugar, and orange
juice in the top part of a glass or enameled double boiler until
thickened, about ten minutes. Add gelatin, stirring to dissolve;
add grated peel. Cool. Beat egg whites until stiff, gradually adding
the one-fourth cup sugar. Fold into the cooked orange mixture.
Spread between the layers of the spongecake and on top. Chill
in the refrigerator. Sprinkle with coconut just before serving, or
decorate with sections of orange. Eight to ten servings.

## RAISIN CAKE

1 cup butter

2 cups sugar

4 eggs

1 cup milk

2½ cups flour

1 teaspoon soda

2 teaspoons cream of tartar

¼ teaspoon nutmeg

1 cup raisins (shaken in a little flour)

Cream butter until soft. Gradually add sugar, creaming until
fluffy, then beat in the eggs. Mix and sift the dry ingredients; add
them to the first mixture alternately with the milk. Add the floured
raisins. Turn into a greased pound-cake pan, and bake in a hot
oven (400 degrees F.) forty-five minutes.

## SEVEN MINUTE FROSTING

2 egg whites, unbeaten               5 tablespoons water
1½ cups sugar                        1½ teaspoons light corn syrup
                    1 teaspoon vanilla

Combine egg whites, sugar, water, and corn syrup in top of double boiler, beating with rotary egg beater until thoroughly mixed. Place over rapidly boiling water, beat constantly with rotary egg beater, and cook seven minutes, or until frosting will stand in peaks. Remove from boiling water; add vanilla, and beat until thick enough to spread. Makes enough frosting to cover tops and sides of two nine-inch layers, tops and sides of three nine-inch layers, or tops and sides of three eight-inch layers.

## FLUFFY SEVEN MINUTE FROSTING

### (USING CORN SYRUP)

2 egg whites, unbeaten               syrup, ½ cup sugar, and
Dash of salt                         5 tablespoons water; or
1 teaspoon vanilla                   ¾ cup light corn syrup,
1½ cups light corn syrup (sub-       ¾ cup sugar, and 5 table-
    stitute 1 cup light corn         spoons water)

Cook as directed for Seven Minute Frosting (above). If frosting separates in the bottom of pan before spreading, beat with rotary egg beater until blended.

## PEPPERMINT FROSTING

Use recipe for Seven Minute Frosting or Fluffy Seven Minute Frosting, substituting one-fourth teaspoon peppermint extract for vanilla. Add green coloring to hot frosting to give a delicate tint. Makes enough frosting for a fifteen-by-ten-inch roll. Or use on layer cake; cover with chocolate coating.

# HUNGARIAN CHOCOLATE FROSTING

3 squares unsweetened chocolate
1½ cups sifted confectioners'
sugar

2½ tablespoons hot water
3 egg yolks
4 tablespoons butter

Melt chocolate in double boiler. Remove from boiling water,
add sugar and water, and blend. Add egg yolks one at a time,
beating well after each. Add butter a tablespoon at a time, beating thoroughly after each amount. Makes enough frosting to
cover tops and sides of two eight-or-nine-inch layers, tops and
sides of two deep nine-inch layers (thinly), or tops and sides of
three nine-inch layers. Or enough to cover top and sides of eight-
by-eight-by-two-inch cake (generously), top and sides of ten-by-
ten-by-two-inch cake, or about two dozen cup cakes. To make
one-half this recipe, use one whole egg, and one-half of all other
ingredients.

# BROWNIES

⅔ cup sifted flour
½ teaspoon baking powder
¼ teaspoon salt
⅓ cup butter or other shortening
1 teaspoon vanilla
2 squares unsweetened chocolate

1 cup sugar (substitute ½ cup
corn syrup or ½ cup
honey and ½ cup sugar.
Bake five to ten minutes
longer)
2 eggs, well beaten
½ cup chopped walnuts or
pecans

Sift flour once, measure, add baking powder and salt, and sift
again. Melt shortening and chocolate over boiling water. Add
sugar gradually to eggs, beating thoroughly; then add chocolate
mixture, and blend. Add flour, and mix well; then add nuts and
vanilla. Decorate with whole nuts, if desired. Bake in greased

pan, eight-by-eight-by-two inches, in moderate oven (350 degrees F.) thirty-five minutes. While still warm, cut in rectangles. Remove from pan and cool on cake rack. Makes two dozen brownies.

## TOASTED COCONUT BROWNIES

Use recipe for Brownies (above), omitting nut meats. Add one cup shredded coconut, finely chopped, to batter. Cover with topping made by mixing thoroughly three-fourths cup coconut with one tablespoon sugar and two teaspoons melted butter. Bake as directed for Brownies.

## CHOCOLATE MACAROONS

2 egg whites
1 cup sugar
¼ teaspoon salt

½ teaspoon vanilla
1½ squares unsweetened chocolate, melted
1½ cups shredded coconut

Beat egg whites until foamy throughout; add sugar, two tablespoons at a time, beating after each addition until sugar is blended. Then continue beating until mixture will stand in peaks. Add salt and vanilla. Fold in chocolate, then coconut. Drop from teaspoon on ungreased heavy paper. Bake in slow oven (325 degrees F.) twenty minutes, or until done. Cook five minutes before removing from paper. Makes two dozen one-and-one-half-inch macaroons.

## LUSCIOUS CHOCOLATE ICEBOX CAKE

3 squares unsweetened chocolate
½ cup sugar
Dash of salt
¼ cup hot water
1 tablespoon cold water

1½ teaspoons granulated gelatin
4 egg yolks
1 teaspoon vanilla
4 egg whites, stiffly beaten
½ cup light cream, whipped
2 dozen ladyfingers

Melt chocolate in top of double boiler. Add sugar, salt, and hot water, stirring until sugar is dissolved and mixture blended. Add cold water to gelatin, and mix. Add to hot chocolate mixture, and stir until gelatin is dissolved; then cook until mixture is smooth and well thickened. Remove from boiling water; add egg yolks one at a time, beating thoroughly after each. Place over boiling water and cook two minutes, stirring constantly. Add vanilla; cool. Fold into egg whites. Chill. Fold in whipped cream.

Line bottom and sides of mold with waxed paper. Arrange ladyfingers on bottom and sides of mold. Add thin layer of thickened chocolate mixture; then arrange ladyfingers and chocolate mixture in alternate layers, topping with chocolate mixture. Cut off ladyfingers around sides of mold, and arrange cut pieces on chocolate mixture. Chill twelve to twenty-four hours in refrigerator. Unmold. Serves eight to ten.

If desired, one-half cup finely cut walnut meats may be added to chocolate mixture before turning into mold. Toast nuts lightly by heating and stirring with a little butter or oil.

## REFRIGERATOR CHEESECAKE

| | |
|---|---|
| 2 eggs | ¾ teaspoon lemon juice |
| ¼ cup milk | ⅔ cup cream, whipped |
| ¾ pound cottage cheese | ½ package zwieback, rolled fine |
| 6 tablespoons sugar | ¼ cup sugar |
| 2 tablespoons flour | ¼ teaspoon cinnamon |
| ¼ teaspoon salt | ⅛ teaspoon salt |
| ½ teaspoon grated lemon rind | 2 tablespoons butter, melted |

Beat eggs, add milk and cottage cheese. Combine sugar, flour, salt, and lemon rind. Add to cheese mixture, and cook in top of double boiler until thick (about ten minutes), stirring occasionally. Remove from fire and add lemon juice. Cool, and fold in whipped cream. Combine zwieback crumbs, sugar, cinnamon, salt, and butter.

Line a loaf pan with waxed paper and arrange cheese and crumb mixtures in alternate layers. Chill in the refrigerator approximately five hours or overnight. Cut in one-inch slices. Serves six to eight.

## ORANGE REFRIGERATOR CAKE

¼ cup orange juice
1 tablespoon gelatin
⅓ cup sugar
½ cup boiling water

¾ cup orange juice
12 marshmallows
¼ cup orange pieces
1 cup whipping cream

24 ladyfingers or a spongecake

Soften gelatin in the one-fourth cup orange juice. Add the sugar and boiling water. Stir to dissolve. Add three-fourths cup orange juice. While gelatin mixture cools, combine marshmallows cut into bits, and orange pieces. When gelatin begins to stiffen, beat until fluffy. Fold in orange pieces, marshmallows, and whipped cream. Line a spring pan with waxed paper. Arrange a layer of ladyfingers (rounded side out) or of spongecake on the bottom and sides. Pour in the filling. Chill in the refrigerator overnight. Unmold and serve plain or garnished with whipped cream and orange sections. Serves eight.

## APRICOT ICE CREAM

¼ cup milk
⅓ cup sugar

⅛ teaspoon salt
1 cup cooked dried apricot pulp

1 cup cream, whipped

Combine milk, sugar, and salt. Mash and strain enough apricots to make one cup of pulp. Add pulp to first mixture, and fold slowly into whipped cream. Pour into freezing tray of the automatic refrigerator and freeze to mushiness; remove from tray and beat thoroughly; then put back in tray to freeze to desired consistency. Six small servings.

## BANANA ICE CREAM

¼ cup milk
¼ cup sugar
⅛ teaspoon salt

1½ teaspoons lemon juice
1 cup mashed bananas
1 cup cream, whipped

Combine milk, sugar, and salt. Combine lemon juice with mashed bananas, and add to first mixture. Fold slowly into whipped cream. Pour into freezing tray of the automatic refrigerator and freeze to mushiness; then remove from tray and beat thoroughly; return to the tray and freeze to the desired consistency. Six small servings.

## BURNT ALMOND ICE CREAM

1 quart cream
1 cup sugar
1 tablespoon vanilla

¼ pound shelled almonds
1 teaspoon caramel
4 tablespoons sherry

Blanch and roast the almonds until golden brown. Pound or chop as fine as possible. Mix sugar and one pint of the cream together, and heat, stirring constantly, until the sugar dissolves. Do not boil. Remove from the fire and add the rest of the cream and the almonds. Let cool. Add caramel, vanilla, and sherry, and freeze in an automatic refrigerator or a freezer.

To make the caramel, put two teaspoons of sugar in a small iron frying pan. Stir over a quick fire with a wooden spoon until the sugar melts and turns amber color. Add one tablespoon boiling water; allow to boil two minutes. Serves six to eight.

## BLACK WALNUT ICE CREAM

¼ cup sugar
⅛ teaspoon salt
¼ cup milk

1 teaspoon vanilla
⅓ cup black walnuts, chopped
　　fine

1 cup whipped cream

Combine sugar, salt, milk, and vanilla. Stir, and add chopped nuts. Fold slowly into whipped cream. Pour into the freezing tray of the automatic refrigerator and freeze to mushiness; remove from the tray, beat thoroughly, and return to the tray to complete freezing. Six small servings.

## DELICIOUS CHOCOLATE ICE CREAM

1½ squares unsweetened choco-
　　late
⅓ cup sugar
Dash of salt

1 cup milk
3 egg yolks, slightly beaten
1 teaspoon vanilla
1 cup light cream, whipped

Add chocolate, sugar, and salt to milk, and heat in double boiler. When chocolate is melted, beat with rotary egg beater until blended. Pour small amount of mixture over egg yolks, stirring vigorously; return to double boiler, and cook two minutes longer, stirring constantly. Chill.

Fold chocolate mixture and vanilla into whipped cream. Turn into freezing tray of automatic refrigerator and let stand three to four hours. Or turn mixture into mold, filling it to overflowing; cover with waxed paper and press cover down tightly. Pack in equal parts of ice and salt for four hours. Makes about three-fourths of a quart.

Note: Two eggs may be substituted for three egg yolks in above recipe. Add egg yolks as directed above. Fold stiffly beaten whites into chilled chocolate before folding into cream.

## OLD-FASHIONED CHOCOLATE ICE CREAM

1 cup sugar
4 tablespoons flour
⅛ teaspoon salt
2 cups milk

3 squares unsweetened chocolate
2 eggs, slightly beaten
4 cups light cream

2 tablespoons vanilla

Combine sugar, flour, and salt in top of double boiler, mixing very thoroughly. Add milk gradually, stirring well. Add chocolate. Place over boiling water; cook and stir until thickened; then continue cooking ten minutes, stirring occasionally. Pour small amount of mixture over eggs, stirring vigorously; return to double boiler, and cook two minutes longer. Cool. Add cream and vanilla. Freeze until stiff, using eight parts ice to one part salt. Remove dasher, and cover tightly; repack in four parts ice to one part salt. Makes two quarts of ice cream.

### COFFEE ICE CREAM

¼ cup sugar
⅛ teaspoon salt
¼ cup strong black freshly made coffee

½ teaspoon vanilla
1 cup cream, whipped

Combine first four ingredients, stir and fold slowly into the whipped cream. Pour into the freezing tray of the automatic refrigerator and freeze to mushiness; remove from the tray and beat thoroughly. Then return to the tray and complete freezing. Six small servings.

### CRANBERRY MOUSSE

1 cup cream
⅛ teaspoon salt

1 cup cranberry sauce, strained

Whip cream, add salt, and fold in strained cranberry sauce

slowly. Pour into freezing tray of the automatic refrigerator, and freeze to desired consistency. Beat thoroughly when half frozen. Serve in sherbet glasses. Serves six.

## ORANGE ICE CREAM

1 cup coffee cream
1 cup sugar
1 cup water
1 cup orange juice

3 tablespoons lemon juice
1 tablespoon grated orange peel

Freeze cream quite firm in a tray of the automatic refrigerator. Bring sugar and water to boiling. Cool; add orange and lemon juice and the grated peel. Freeze. Whip the frozen cream. Beat the frozen mixture. Combine with the cream and continue freezing. Serves six.

## PISTACHIO ICE CREAM

¼ cup sugar
⅛ teaspoon salt
½ teaspoon pistachio flavoring
½ teaspoon vanilla

Few drops green coloring
¼ cup milk
½ cup pistachio nuts, cut fine
1 cup cream, whipped

Combine sugar, salt, flavorings, coloring, and milk. Stir well, and add nuts. Fold slowly into whipped cream. Pour into the freezing tray of your automatic refrigerator and freeze to thick mush consistency. Remove from the tray and beat thoroughly with a spoon; return to tray and let freeze to ice cream firmness. Six small servings.

## ORANGE SHERBET

1 tablespoon gelatin
2 tablespoons cold water
1½ cups sugar
1 cup water

2 egg whites
2 tablespoons sugar
2 cups orange juice
3 tablespoons lemon juice

Soften gelatin in two tablespoons water. Boil the one and one-half cups sugar and one cup water five minutes to make a syrup. Dissolve gelatin mixture in the hot syrup. Beat the egg whites until frothy, and add the two tablespoons sugar. Continue beating until stiff. Beat the syrup into the egg whites slowly, then mix in fruit juices. Pour into the freezing tray of the automatic refrigerator, and set the cold control for fast freezing. After it has partially frozen, turn into a cold bowl and beat until blended and fluffy. Return to the refrigerator to freeze again. Beat every thirty minutes until the mixture holds its shape. This makes about one quart, six to eight servings. Freezing time, five to six hours.

## SAUCES

In both the casserole and chafing dish recipes, sauces play an important rôle. The most frequently used sauce in American cookery is the white sauce, but in recent years, as American housekeepers have learned more about various kinds of European cookery, many of our recipes have gradually changed and boldly called for more elaborate sauces which once were the exclusive creations of famous chefs.

These concoctions have been simplified in America, and as used in our cookery actually are no more difficult to make than the white sauce every American girl learns in grade-school cooking classes. If the recipe calls for an unusual herb or condiment, it is easy in most parts of this country to find that ingredient—and eminently worth while because the sauce is the better for it.

Don't be casual about sauces; make the basic ones according to the recipe and, as called for in many recipes in this book, step it up with flavoring, herb, spice, yolk of egg, browned flour, cream, or anything else demanded. The final flavor of some dishes depends on the sauce.

## WHITE SAUCE

1 tablespoon butter      1 cup milk
1 tablespoon flour      ¼ teaspoon salt
⅛ teaspoon pepper or paprika

## MEDIUM WHITE SAUCE

2 tablespoons butter      1 cup milk
2 tablespoons flour      ¼ teaspoon salt
⅛ teaspoon pepper or paprika

## THICK WHITE SAUCE

3 to 4 tablespoons butter      1 cup milk
3 to 4 tablespoons flour      ¼ teaspoon salt
     ⅛ teaspoon pepper or paprika

The procedure for all is the same. Melt the butter, add flour, and stir smoothly until blended and perfectly smooth. Then add the milk a little at a time, and cook over gentle heat, stirring constantly, continuing to cook several minutes after the sauce boils. Season at the end. Best results with a double boiler.

## CHEESE SAUCE

Add to scalding hot Medium White Sauce five to six tablespoons grated cheese, and beat thoroughly.

## FRENCH WHITE SAUCE OR CREAM SAUCE

This sauce is sometimes called Cream Sauce, or properly, French White Sauce, in contrast to the simple American version made with flour, butter, milk, and seasoned only with salt and a little pepper. French White Sauce adds richness and flavor to any mixture in which it is called for. In certain recipes it may be called Cream Sauce.

In place of stock, which most housekeepers do not have the time to make (and in these days the meat), use bouillon cubes or canned bouillon. But it is only fair to tell you that it is from well-made and carefully seasoned stock that the subtle and improved flavor of the sauce (and the dish in which it is used) comes.

3 tablespoons butter      Salt, pepper, nutmeg
3 tablespoons flour      1 teaspoon lemon juice
     1½ cups stock

Melt the butter, and stir the flour smoothly into it until thick and smooth. Do not allow it to brown. Add the stock a little at a time, stirring it smoothly into the butter and flour mixture. When well thickened, season with salt and pepper and just a few grains of nutmeg. Add the lemon juice, mix through the sauce, and it is ready to use.

## BÉARNAISE SAUCE

3 tablespoons tarragon vinegar
¼ tablespoon chopped shallot
Coarsely ground pepper
2 egg yolks
¼ pound butter, melted
1 dessertspoon chopped chervil
　　and tarragon

Put the tarragon vinegar in a glass or enamel saucepan with the chopped shallot and a shake of coarsely ground pepper. Reduce this to about two dessertspoonfuls. Let it get nearly cold; then stir in the beaten yolks of the eggs, and thicken by adding over low heat the melted butter. Strain through muslin, taste, and correct the seasoning to suit your taste. Finish by adding the chopped chervil and tarragon leaves. Makes about one cup.

## BÉCHAMEL SAUCE I

1 tablespoon butter
1½ tablespoons flour
Nutmeg
1 onion, with clove stuck in it
1¾ cups milk
¼ teaspoon salt
Bouquet of parsley, thyme, and bay leaf

Melt the butter, and stir the flour smoothly into it; add the scalding hot milk, and season with the salt and grated nutmeg; bring to boiling, stirring all the time. Then add the bouquet of parsley and herbs, and simmer gently for ten minutes. Remove the bouquet, and continue cooking and stirring until slightly thickened. Let cool. It thickens more as it cools. Makes one cup.

## BÉCHAMEL SAUCE II

3 tablespoons butter
3 tablespoons flour
½ small onion

¾ cup stock (or bouillon cube)
¼ cup cream
Salt and pepper

Make as for French White Sauce, adding the cream after the stock and thickening have been blended. Add the onion while the sauce is cooking, but remove before serving.

## MORNAY SAUCE I

Three tablespoons grated Gruyère and Parmesan cheese added to Béchamel Sauce, the sauce reheated long enough to melt the cheese, and you have Mornay Sauce. If the Mornay Sauce is put on top of a casserole mixture which is to go back into the oven a few minutes, the sauce need not be heated after the cheese is added.

## MORNAY SAUCE II

¼ pint Béchamel Sauce
2 egg yolks
Cream
2 tablespoons grated Parmesan

and Gruyère cheese
mixed
2 tablespoons butter
Bouillon from fish or chicken

To the Béchamel Sauce add, while it is boiling, a binding of the two egg yolks and the mixed cheese. Then add a few spoonfuls of either chicken bouillon or the broth from a cooked fish (for which the sauce is intended), and the same number of spoonfuls of cream with two tablespoons of butter. Mix smoothly; serve at once. About one and one-half cups.

## HORSERADISH SAUCE

2 tablespoons freshly grated
horseradish

½ cup butter
1 tablespoon lemon juice

Whip the butter to a cream, gradually beating in the horse-radish, then the lemon juice. Keep on the ice until ready to serve. Spread on hot fillets of meat. Enough for six servings.

## MINT SAUCE

1 bunch mint (eight to ten
   stalks)
¼ cup boiling water

1 to 2 tablespoons sugar
1 lemon, juice only
¼ teaspoon salt
¼ teaspoon pepper

Wash the mint and shake dry on a cloth. Pick the leaves from the stems, and chop very fine. Add the boiling water and sugar, cover closely, and let stand for half an hour. Add the lemon juice and seasonings. Used with lamb. Almost one cup.

## SPECIAL TARTARE SAUCE

1 cup mayonnaise
2 tablespoons capers
2 tablespoons olives

2 tablespoons gherkins,
   chopped fine
½ chili pepper
½ cup double cream

Chop the capers, olives, gherkins, and pepper exceedingly fine. Beat the cream stiff. When ready to serve the sauce, fold the prepared vegetables and whipped cream into the mayonnaise. About two cups.

## CURRANT JELLY SAUCE

1 slice onion
2 slices carrot
6 peppercorns
¼ bay leaf
1 sprig parsley

2 tablespoons butter
3 tablespoons flour
1 cup bouillon
Salt and pepper
¼ cup currant jelly
2 tablespoons Madeira wine

Brown the first five ingredients in the butter; add the flour and brown; then add the stock and stir till boiling; add the jelly and wine. Beat thoroughly, and strain. About two cups.

## HOT ORANGE SAUCE

1 orange, peel and juice
1½ oranges, juice only
¾ cup brown stock (or bouillon)

1 lemon, juice only
¼ teaspoon salt
¼ teaspoon cayenne

Cut the peel into tiny shreds, and cover with boiling water. Cook five minutes, then drain. To the blanched peel, add the other ingredients and stir until hot; then serve. Makes two cups.

## WINE SAUCE

3 cups water
1½ cups sugar

1 lemon, grated rind and juice
2 teaspoons cornstarch

¼ cup cognac or kirsch

Place water and sugar, lemon rind and juice in a glass or enameled saucepan. Bring to boiling, and add the cornstarch which has been dissolved in a little cold water. Stir, and bring again to boiling. Add the wine. Strain. Enough for four to six desserts.

## COFFEE AND TEA

Make your coffee according to the directions which come with the pot you are using. Buy the best coffee you can find, and experiment with different brands and pots until you find the blend and the coffee maker which produce the results you like. Coffee is a highly individual affair—some like it black and strong, aromatic and free from chicory; some like it full of chicory, as in the Italian and French restaurants, and black-roasted at that. Many today prefer the decaffeinated coffee which is made according to directions for any coffee.

In your own kitchen, after you have found the mixture and the coffee maker which seem perfect, give your careful attention to the care of the device and to making each brew.

Glass coffee makers, which can be washed spotless and odorless with hot water, and china and pottery drip combinations, with the same happy reaction to clean hot water, are probably the most satisfactory for many housekeepers. There need be no taste of an oft-used filter or of a poorly cleaned pot with these. This immaculate freedom from echoes of past coffee-making is essential to good coffee. The pot must be surgically clean.

Use fresh coffee—freshly roasted and freshly ground, if you can get it; the vacuum-packed coffee is the next best thing.

Select the grind suited to the special coffee maker you use.

Use enough coffee. The generally accepted rule is one heaping tablespoon per standard measuring cup of water. For after-dinner coffee and iced coffee, use double this amount.

Make coffee just before it is served. Don't make it while the dinner is cooking, intending to keep it hot until used. Only freshly made coffee has both aroma and body—two factors in flavor.

Follow the directions on the coffee maker you use.

## DRIP COFFEE

Scald pot. Place measured coffee in its compartment and add freshly boiled measured water. Cover, and let stand where the coffee will keep hot until all water has dripped through. Serve at once.

## GLASS COFFEE MAKER

Fill the bottom compartment with the right amount of water and bring to boiling. Place the upper part of the glass coffee maker, with the measured coffee in it, correctly in the opening of the lower half. Adjust. Let the water go up once through the coffee; stir. Remove the device from the heat and let the coffee pass down into the lower half. Then remove the upper half. Pour the coffee directly into a scalded pot for living room service; or use this glass container for service.

## PERCOLATED COFFEE

Measure water (cold or boiling, as preferred) into the lower compartment of a spotlessly clean and freshly scalded percolator. Set the coffee basket in position, put measured coffee in it, and cover. Place over low heat, and let percolate, slowly at first, ten to fifteen minutes depending on the type of percolator used and the strength of coffee desired.

## BOILED COFFEE

Combine measured cold water and coffee, and bring slowly to boiling, stirring occasionally. Then remove from the fire; pour in a very little cold water to settle the grounds. Let stand three to five minutes; then serve.

If you use boiling water, combine with the coffee, let boil up rapidly two or three times, and settle with cold water. Let stand, and serve.

## FOR AFTER-DINNER COFFEE

Use any preferred method, but double the amount of the coffee.

## TEA

Make tea in an earthen, glass, or china teapot. Scald; measure the tea into it. Allow almost a teaspoon to each cup, according to the quality of the tea and the strength preferred. Add freshly boiling water, infuse three to five minutes, strain, and pour.

Study the different kinds of tea to learn their unique flavors and strengths. Some black teas are so strong that one-half teaspoon for each cup is sufficient.

For iced tea, make a strong brew using about twice as much tea as for the hot beverage. Pour, when freshly made, over cracked ice or cubes in a tall glass.

# INDEX

SALADS, 119
Artichoke Hearts and Tomato, 122
Asparagus Vinaigrette, 121
Carrot and Potato, 122
Chef's California Salad Bowl, 122
Coleslaw (2 recipes), 123
Cucumber Cream, 123
Endive, 124
Garden, 124
Grapefruit Perfection, 125
Grapefruit Starter, 126
Orange Cranberry Relish, 124
Potato, 125
Romaine and Grapefruit, 126
Royal, 126
Southern Chicken, 127
Spring Salad Platter, 128
Tossed Green, 128
Western Fruit Plate, 127
SAUCES, 168
Béarnaise, 170
Béchamel (2 recipes), 170
Cheese, 169
Cream, 169
Currant Jelly, 172
Horseradish, 171
Mint, 172
Madeira, 111
Mornay (2 recipes), 171
Orange, 173
Tartare, 172
White (4 recipes), 168
Wine, 173
Sausage Meat with Baked Apples, 77
Sausage with Sweet Potato Topping, 78
Savory Potatoes, 92
Scalloped Eggs and Shrimp, 39
Scalloped Fish, 32
Scalloped Ham, 71
Scalloped Lima Beans, 86
Scalloped Liver and Potatoes, 75
Scalloped Mushrooms, 93
Scalloped Oysters and Scallops, 38
Scalloped Peas and Eggs, 94

Scalloped Sweet Potatoes and Apples, 96
Scrambled Eggs, 118
Shepherd's Pie, 78
Sherberts (See ICE CREAMS)
Shirred Eggs in Macaroni, 46
Short Ribs Barbecued, 76
Shrimp and Macaroni, 41
Shrimp and Rice au Gratin, 41
Shrimp and Rice Casserole, 40
Shrimp Bake, 42
Shrimp, Clubman's, 116
Shrimp Pie, 39
Shrimp Soufflé, 40
Shrimp Tomato Casserole, 42
Smothered Chicken, 59
Sole with Herbs, 34
SOUP IN CASSEROLE MENUS, 20
SOUPS, 22
Black Bean, 22
Clam Chowder, 23
Leek and Potato, 23
Lentil, 23
Minestrone, 24
Mulligatawny, 22
Onion au Gratin, 24
Pepperpot, 25
Pot-au-Feu, 25
Sour Cream Dressing, 132
Southern Chicken Salad, 127
Southern Soufflé, 147
Spaghetti and Tomato Casserole, 52
SPAGHETTI IN CASSEROLE MENUS, 47
Spanish Turkey, 61
Spinach au Gratin, 95
Spoon Bread, 53
Spring Salad Platter, 128
Strawberry Shortcake, Old-Fashioned, 146
Strawberry-Raspberry Dessert, 147
Stuffed Baked Onions, 93
Sugar Substitutes, 152
Swedish Apple Pudding, 134
Swedish Fish Soufflé, 35
Sweetbreads, Creamed with Mushrooms, 78
Sweetbreads in Casserole, 77
Sweet Potato Pudding, 96